Praise for Rick Shenkman's
Just How Stupid Are We?

◆

"What Shenkman does not do is chortle, Mencken-like,
about stupidity. He offers plausible suggestions for how the
knowledge level of the American electorate might be raised
to a respectable threshold."

—*Newsweek.com*

"Shenkman combines his talents as a reporter and a historian
to assess why the American voter can be rational and yet so
capable of "being played like a fiddle" by politicians . . .
highly recommended."

—*Library Journal*

"In lucid, playful prose . . . Shenkman initiates an important
conversation in this book and makes welcome suggestions
to reinvigorate civic responsibility and provide people
with the knowledge and tools necessary to efficaciously
participate in the political process."

—*Publishers Weekly*

"With wit, passion and devastating evidence, Shenkman
compels us, the praised and petted 'American people,' to

look in the mirror for an explanation of why our elections are travesties of informed, intelligent debate. Lively and crucial, the book reminds us, however we vote, that there's no such animal as 'democracy for dummies.'"

—BERNARD A. WEISBERGER, author of *America Afire*

"The bad news is that Americans are ignorant, short-sighted, and swayed by meaningless phrases; the good news is that things could get better—if we start speaking honestly about the problem. Rick Shenkman's book is a crucial starting point in that process."

—JON WIENER, Professor of History
at University of California at Irvine
and author of *Historians in Trouble*

"Are manipulative politicians and an intimidated media the only reasons we've had to suffer through the Bush years? What about the American people? Why don't they stop, pay attention, and think for themselves? In his candid and hard-hitting history of American political culture, Shenkman offers a compelling and disturbing analysis of the American people and why we get the government we deserve."

—RUTH ROSEN, Professor Emerita of History,
University of California, Davis

Just How Stupid Are We?

Just How Stupid Are We?

*Facing the Truth About
the American Voter*

RICK SHENKMAN

A Member of the Perseus Books Group
New York

The Library of Congress has catalogued the hardcover edition as
follows:
Shenkman, Richard.
    Just how stupid are we? : facing the truth about the American
voter / Rick Shenkman.
        p. cm.
    ISBN 978-0-465-07771-7 (alk. paper)
    1. Political participation—United States—History—21st century.
2. Political culture—United States—History—21st century. 3.
United States—Politics and government—2001- 4. United States—
Civilization—21st century. I. Title.

JK1764.S534 2008
320.973—dc22

                                                        2007052601

Paperback ISBN: 978-0-465-01493-4
10 9 8 7 6 5 4 3 2 1

FOR JOHN STUCKY

MAGGIE: Truth! Truth! Everybody keeps hollerin' about the truth. Well, the truth is as dirty as lies.

BRICK: Can you face the truth . . . ?

BIG DADDY: Try me!

BRICK: You or somebody else's truth?

BIG DADDY: Bull. You're runnin' again.

BRICK: Yeah, I am runnin'. Runnin' from lies, lies like birthday congratulations and many happy returns of the day when there won't be any.

—*Cat on a Hot Tin Roof*

Contents

◆

Author's Note

◆

After The Bad Bush Years there is a deep yearning in America for change. Many of us cannot wait for the head-line: "George W. Bush Leaves Office." Along with millions of Americans, throngs around the world will no doubt cheer the news of his departure, as will I.

But as the reader will see, I am convinced that it is too easy to blame our mess on Mr. Bush. And I do not believe that his replacement by a leader who is less partisan and more competent and sensitive to civil liberties will begin to remedy what ails us.

What went wrong, went wrong long before Mr. Bush's ascendancy. His flaws simply gave us the unwelcome op-portunity of seeing what heretofore had remained largely invisible.

We have had enough books about Mr. Bush, and I, for one, frankly am tired of them. What we need now are books to help us understand *us*. What has happened did not happen as a result of a single leader's mistakes. We had a hand in it.

The cliché is that people get the government they deserve. If that's true, why did we deserve Mr. Bush?

That is the question I set out to answer.

RICK SHENKMAN
Seattle

1

The Problem

◆

The great enemy of the truth is very often not the lie—
deliberate, contrived, and dishonest, but the myth—
persistent, persuasive, and unrealistic. Belief in myths
allows the comfort of opinion without the discomfort
of thought.
—JOHN F. KENNEDY

Are America's voters prepared to shoulder the responsibility of running the most powerful nation on earth? Do a majority know enough? Care enough? Think hard and clearly enough?

A sign of our self-confidence as a people is that we regularly call attention to the dumb things our politicians say and do. But who takes the voters to task for *their* foolishness? Any dolt can make fun of a politician. What if the real problem isn't with them but with us—or, to be more precise, those among us who exhibit habitual stupidity?

To be blunt: We are, it seems to me, guilty of a certain kind of cowardice for our failure to inquire deeply into the mistakes the voters make. Even after 9/11, when fresh thinking was needed most, we neglected as a society to confront harsh truths about the limits of the public's wisdom. Busy spreading democracy around the world, we refused to reflect bravely on the defects of our own. Instead of admitting our flaws, we settled, somewhat defensively, on the myth that we are a good and great people with noble aims.

The willingness to address our myths calls for a certain amount of courage. The thesis of this book is that courage of the sort we need has been in short supply of late. We have allowed the myth of The People to warp our politics, limit the choices of our leaders, and hinder us in our war with Islamist terrorists, putting our democracy, and possibly even our lives, in danger. While pundits on both the Left and the Right have advanced vigorous arguments about a seemingly endless number of hot topics, they have largely ignored how the voters' limitations have sabotaged us time and again. One of the purposes of this book is to provide various ways to have a constructive conversation about this most sensitive of subjects.

Presumably most Americans would agree that honesty and clear-headedness are desirable. So why has it been so difficult for us to achieve these twin goals? The conclusion I have reached is that we may not truly desire the truth, however sincerely we believe that we do. The record of our history suggests that, given a choice between a harsh truth and a comforting myth, we have been inclined to embrace the latter.

We flatter ourselves that we are, in the wake of 9/11, a serious people—or, at any rate, a *more* serious people than formerly. But seriousness surely means, if it means anything, the willingness to face facts, even those facts that may give us a bad case of indigestion. And this, as we shall see, we have not been willing to do.

Our problem is twofold. Not only are we often blind to the faults of the voters, owing to the myth of The People, but the voters themselves frequently base their opinions on myths. This is a terrible conundrum. Democracy is rooted in the assumption that we are creatures of reason. If instead, as seems likely, we human beings are hardwired to mythologize events and our own history, we are left with the paradox that our confidence in democracy rests on a myth.

Of all our myths, I believe the myth of The People to be the most dangerous one confronting us at present. The evidence of the last few years that millions are grossly ignorant of the basic facts involving the most important issues we face has brought me to this sad conclusion. As became irrefutably clear in scientific polls undertaken after 9/11 by the Program on International Policy Attitudes (PIPA), millions of Americans simply cannot fathom the twists and turns that complicated debates take.

In January 2003, three months before our invasion of Iraq, the survey-takers found that a majority of Americans falsely believed that "Iraq played an important role in 9/11." Over the next year and a half PIPA polls indicated that a persistent 57 percent believed that Saddam Hussein was helping al Qaeda at the time we were attacked. (Other polls came up with higher numbers. For instance, in September 2003 a *Washington Post* poll found that 70 percent of Americans believed Saddam was personally involved in the 9/11 attacks.) In the spring of 2004 the 9/11 Commission flatly stated that Saddam had not provided support to al Qaeda. The Commission's findings received saturation coverage. Nonetheless, in August of the same year, according to a PIPA poll, 50 percent were still insisting that Saddam had given "substantial" support to al Qaeda. (A full two years later, in 2006, a Zogby International poll indicated that 46 percent of Americans continued to believe that "there is a link between Saddam Hussein and the 9/11 terrorist attacks.")

The illusion that Saddam was behind 9/11 had real-world consequences. A poll for *Investor's Business Daily* and the *Christian Science Monitor* cited by the PIPA researchers found that 80 percent of those who backed the Iraq War in 2003 said that a key reason for their support was their belief that Saddam had ties to al Qaeda.

Another clear indication of public ignorance concerned the claim that Saddam possessed "weapons of mass destruction," which became such a ubiquitous part of the national conversation that the phrase soon became known by its initials: WMD. Poll results show that the voters were quick to absorb the administration line, but only slowly came to realize that they had been snowed.* As late as the spring of 2004 a clear majority remained unaware that experts such as Hans Blix (head of the UN weapons inspectors), David Kay (the former head of the Iraq Survey Group), and Richard Clarke (the national coordinator

---

*Some may question my use of the word *snowed*. Supporters of the Bush administration insist that the concern with WMD was, though ultimately proven inaccurate, sincere. They note that even President Clinton was convinced that Saddam possessed WMD. President Bush himself reportedly still believed the claim as late as 2006, according to biographer Robert Draper's *Dead Certain: The Presidency of George W. Bush* (Free Press, 2007). But the administration's apologists cannot defend the numerous misleading statements made about Saddam's alleged nuclear program—and it was these claims that most frightened the American public. For instance, on October 7, 2002, President Bush claimed in a speech that Saddam had attempted to purchase aluminum tubes designed to enrich uranium. This statement was in flat contradiction of the findings of the government's own experts at the Department of Energy, who had concluded the tubes were not suitable for the enrichment of uranium—a conclusion included in the National Intelligence Estimate provided to Congress the same month. (See *Media Matters for America*, April 23, 2007, available online at www.mediamatters.org/items/20070423004.) In 2003, three days before the invasion of Iraq, in an appearance on *Meet the Press*, Vice President Cheney insisted that Saddam "has, in fact, reconstituted nuclear weapons." Cheney's statement was in contradiction of the findings of Mohamed ElBaradei, the director of the UN's International Atomic Energy Agency, but Cheney insisted, "I think Mr. ElBaradei frankly is wrong." ElBaradei, of course, was right. A more circumspect official in Cheney's position would have admitted he had no evidence to back up his suspicions. But Cheney was interested in making a case for war. He therefore did not let on that all he had were suspicions, not facts.

for counterterrorism) had firmly concluded that Iraq lacked WMD at the time of our invasion, even though their findings had received wide publicity.

Finally, there was the question of world opinion. By all measures the Iraq War was unpopular around the world. On the eve of the war millions protested, bitterly denouncing George W. Bush and the United States. In several countries these were the largest anti-American rallies ever held. Opposition was strong even in countries that were traditional American allies, such as Spain. Most Americans, however, did not comprehend the isolation of the United States. According to PIPA, the majority either believed that world opinion was about evenly divided or actually favored the war (31 percent were in the second camp). Only 35 percent realized that the planned invasion had drawn far more criticism than support.

Given all this, a robust debate about public opinion would seem warranted. If Americans cannot think straight about events of the magnitude of 9/11 and the Iraq War, what can they think straight about? But no such debate has been forthcoming. Instead, we have had endless arguments about the media and the nefariousness of the Bush administration. Both of these arguments have merit, in my opinion. But they were never pushed far enough to get to the real problem.

Take the debate about the media. It focused almost wholly on statistics indicating that Fox News viewers were far more likely to hold misinformed opinions about both 9/11 and Iraq than people who relied on other sources of information. These statistics *were* alarming. According to the PIPA researchers, 80 percent of regular Fox News viewers held erroneous impressions about Saddam's ties to al Qaeda and his possession of WMD. In contrast, only 23 percent of those who followed the news on the Public Broadcasting System and National Public Radio were similarly misinformed. Fox viewers were also more likely than the PBS/NPR audience to believe that world opinion favored the Iraq War. But these findings, interesting as they are, prove only that the media played a critical role in forming public opinion. They do not tell us why the public passively absorbed false information. Worse, by focusing on these findings in the way that many critics did—placing emphasis on the media's failures rather than on those of the public—the critics left the impression that the public was an innocent bystander. Because the debate was limited in this fashion, voters did not come in for the criticism they deserved.

The other argument critics made was that the Bush administration played on Americans' fears and misled them with misinformation. Like the argument about the media, this one was true. Evidence abounds that President George W. Bush, Vice President Dick Cheney, and political consultant Karl Rove repeatedly exploited the fear of 9/11 terrorism. During the 2004 campaign Cheney brazenly suggested that if John Kerry were elected the United States likely would face another attack. Tom

Ridge, the first head of the Department of Homeland Security, admitted in 2005 that the administration periodically raised security threat levels based on flimsy evidence and over his objections. The public got the false impression that Saddam was in league with al Qaeda because administration officials explicitly said so. In December 2001 Cheney, in an appearance on *Meet the Press*, said "it's been pretty well confirmed" that 9/11 hijacker Mohamed Atta had met "with a senior official of the Iraqi intelligence service in Czechoslovakia last April, several months before the attack." But while highlighting the Bush administration's manipulation should we not also wonder about the public's susceptibility to it? Plenty has been said about the deceivers, but little about the deceived. Why were so many people deceivable?

Our reluctance to entertain questions about public opinion is both strange and singular. In all previous periods of American history the expression of doubts about The People has been a marked feature of mainstream public debate. In response to the widespread use of propaganda by both the Allies and the Central Powers in World War I, so-called nervous liberals such as Walter Lippmann worried that ordinary people left to their own devices could easily be led astray by demagogues. In place of the "barbarism" of mass democracy Lippmann recommended that experts (he had himself in mind) be given the responsibility for guiding public opinion. John Dewey, though ostensibly an optimist, presciently warned that in a consumer society, which at the time had not yet fully materialized, voters would be hard-pressed to fulfill their responsibilities as citizens given the available distractions. A people who spend their evenings attending movies, listening to the radio, and taking automobile rides would take less interest in politics, making them increasingly vulnerable to manipulation, he predicted. And then there were the fears that popped up in the 1930s when liberals anxiously worried about the appeal that fascism might have to the vast armies of the unemployed.

Happily, Americans did not turn toward fascism, but events in our own time have confirmed the broad outlines of the indictment Lippmann and Dewey made. Shockingly, however, elites in the country have not seized the moment of the Iraq disaster to educate the public about the frighteningly large dimensions of the failure of millions to absorb basic facts about critical issues. While some critics who had warned against the invasion from the beginning have played the unhelpful "I told you so" game, and others have chronicled the step-by-step mistakes the administration made, virtually none have explored what the public's approval of the war on the basis of misinformation says about the maturity of our democracy. In the media, if not in the academy, thoughtful questions about the wisdom of The People have been met with near dead silence. (The contempt for ordinary voters frequently expressed by left-wing bloggers distressed by the victories of President Bush and the Republicans in

2002 and 2004 does not count. The bloggers offered a sneer, not a critique.)

We have more reason to worry than the "nervous liberals" that large groups of American voters can be swung with demagogic appeals. Whereas in the twentieth century fascism did not come to the United States, in the twenty-first, rank appeals to fear based on misinformation succeeded in winning the support of an overwhelming majority of Americans. In the 1930s the critics based their analyses upon what they worried *might* happen. Our situation is more dire. We know that in fact the masses *can* be moved by fear and misinformation, because they were. The critics in the '30s overestimated the dangers they imagined; the likelihood that America would turn fascist was slight. But we refuse to admit that what has happened, happened.

Experience teaches us that we can muddle through despite the serious deficiencies in the American public's capacities. But complacency may not be warranted. Over the last four decades American politics has become increasingly democratic, putting more and more power directly into the hands of ordinary voters. Nothing in our past experience justifies the belief that people in these circumstances are up to the task that history has now given them.

I am not, however, pessimistic. Reform of both ourselves and our system is plausible as well as desirable, as I point out in the final chapter of this book. If we want a country of smart voters who can't be played like a fiddle we can certainly have one. I, for one, know that's the kind of country in which I want to live.

Before proceeding further I should point out that myths are not synonymous with lies. Some myths supply a needed grand narrative to help us define who we are and what values we cherish. As I have written elsewhere, I would no sooner want to dispense with the George Washington myth than I would want to take Santa Claus out and shoot him. A world without myths is inconceivable.

My goal here is not to abolish myths. It is, rather, to draw attention to them. Once we can see them they lose their power to twist and confine our thinking. With regard to the myth of The People, what needs explaining is how we arrived at the point where voters could get so much wrong about 9/11 and Iraq without there being a sustained public debate about their responsibility for the situation. In the remainder of this book I will try to explain how this happened.

Our generation is not unique in having to face its myths. Every generation of Americans has had to do the same, as various challenges presented themselves. Nor is our failure to deal with the myths of our own time conspicuous. Failure has been more common than success in these kinds of efforts in American history. But it is worth remembering that failure is not inevitable. On occasion, Americans, acting under pressure, have cast off dangerous and beguiling myths, as we did during the Civil War under the leadership of Abraham Lincoln, who in 1862 memorably told Congress it was time to consider freeing the country's slaves: "The dogmas of the quiet past, are inadequate to the stormy present. The occasion is piled high with difficulty, and we must rise—with the occasion. As our case is new, so we must think anew, and act anew. We must disenthrall ourselves, and then we shall save our country."

2

Gross Ignorance

◆

If a nation expects to be ignorant and free, in a state of
civilization, it expects what never was and never will be.
— THOMAS JEFFERSON

Just how stupid are we? Pretty stupid, it would seem,
when we come across headlines like this: "Homer Simpson, Yes—1st Amendment 'Doh,' Survey Finds."

About 1 in 4 Americans can name more than one of the five
freedoms guaranteed by the First Amendment (freedom of
speech, religion, press, assembly, and petition for redress of
grievances). But more than half of Americans can name at
least two members of the fictional cartoon family, according to a survey.

The study by the new McCormick Tribune Freedom
Museum found that 22 percent of Americans could name
all five Simpson family members, compared with just 1 in

1,000 people who could name all five First Amendment freedoms.
—Associated Press, March 1, 2006

But what does it mean, exactly, to say that The People are stupid? About this there is unfortunately no consensus. Like Supreme Court Justice Potter Stewart, who confessed to not knowing how to define *pornography*, we are apt simply to throw up our hands in frustration and say: We know it when we see it. But unless we attempt a definition of some sort we risk incoherence, dooming our investigation of stupidity from the outset. Stupidity cannot mean, as Humpty Dumpty would have it, whatever we say it means.

Five defining characteristics of stupidity, it seems to me, are readily apparent. First is sheer ignorance: ignorance of critical facts about important events in the news, and ignorance of how our government functions and who's in charge. Second is negligence: the disinclination to seek reliable sources of information about important news events. Third is wooden-headedness, as the historian Barbara Tuchman defined it: the inclination to believe what we want to believe, regardless of the facts. Fourth is shortsightedness: the support of public policies that are mutually exclusive, or contrary to the country's long-term interests. Fifth, and finally, is a broad category I call bone-headedness, for want of a better word: the susceptibility to meaningless phrases, stereotypes, irrational biases, and simplistic diagnoses and solutions that play on our hopes and fears.

The problem with a list like this is that it raises as many questions as it is designed to answer. What is fact and not fact is often unclear. The use of bad judgment is not clearly distinguishable from stupidity. Which sources of information are reliable is frequently a matter of subjective judgment, with liberals and conservatives reaching different conclusions. One man's "empty slogan" can be another's inspiring bon mot. Further, stereotyping is a function of time and place. A white voter who stereotypes blacks today would probably be considered stupid in many quarters, but not two centuries ago in the era of the Founding Fathers, when racial prejudice was nearly universal. Norms change. And it would be foolish to try to pretend that they don't and that standards of stupidity can be applied abstractly across the generations.

It is obvious that all of us are likely to be guilty of stupidity from time to time. This is worth remembering. Doing so may help save us from drawing too harsh a judgment about the public. We cannot demand that the masses should meet a standard that is beyond the grasp of any one of us individually.

Having defined stupidity—more or less—we face another problem: measuring and assessing it. We usually measure public opinion through the use of polls. Assuming the polls are accurate (which itself is problematic as polls are often misleading, either because the questions are poorly phrased or because the sample is unrepresentative), how do we assess the findings? If, say, half the respondents do not know that the Constitution was drafted in Philadelphia, as happens to be the case, does that entitle one to conclude that The People are stupid? Or is a higher percentage required—say, 51 percent? And if we are to grade the public in this manner, what shall we say constitutes a passing or failing grade? Must The People answer ten out of ten questions incorrectly to be given a failing grade? Eight out of ten? Six out of ten? I do not believe that there is a neat and tidy answer to the question I have posed. It is perhaps enough just to ask the question. For by asking it we readily glean just how complex this whole subject of public stupidity is. And as a starting point that's a pretty good one. This book is not intended to provide a definitive answer to the question of how stupid we are. I would be happy simply to help make the question a part of our everyday public debate.

Taking up the first of our definitions of stupidity, how ignorant are we? Ask the political scientists and you will be told that there is damning, hard evidence pointing incontrovertibly to the conclusion that millions are embarrassingly ill-informed and that they do not care that they are. There is enough evidence that one could almost conclude—though admittedly this is a stretch—that we are living in an Age of Ignorance.

Surprised? My guess is most people would be. Like the students I encountered in 2004 as I was giving lectures on college campuses about the coming presidential election, the general impression seems to be that we are living in an age in which people are particularly knowledgeable. Many students told me that they are the most well-informed generation in history.

Why are we so deluded? The error can be traced to our mistaking unprecedented access to information with the actual consumption of it. Our access to information is indeed phenomenal. George Washington had to wait two weeks to discover that he had been elected president of the United States. That's how long it took for the news to travel from New York, where the Electoral College votes were counted, to his home in Mount Vernon, Virginia. Americans living in the interior regions had to wait even longer, some up to two months. Now we can watch developments as they occur halfway around the world in real time. It is little wonder, then, that students boast of their knowledge. Unlike their parents, who were forced to rely mainly on newspapers and the network news shows to find out what was happening in the world, they can flip on CNN and Fox or consult the Internet.

But in fact only a small percentage of people take advantage of the great new resources at hand. In 2005 the Pew Research Center surveyed the news habits of some 3,000 Americans age 18 and older. The researchers found that 59 percent on a regular basis get at least some news from local TV, 47 percent from national TV news shows, and just 23 percent from the Internet.

Anecdotal evidence suggested for years that Americans were not particularly well-informed. As foreign visitors long ago observed, Americans are vastly inferior in their knowledge of world geography compared with Europeans. (The old joke is that "war is God's way of teaching Americans geography.") And while Europeans have long known what is happening politically on this side of the ocean, few Americans bother to find out what is happening politically on their side. Only a small minority of Americans—about 20 percent—even hold a passport. But it was never clear until the postwar period just how ignorant Americans are. For it was only then that social scientists began measuring in a systematic manner what Americans actually know. The results were devastating.

The most comprehensive surveys, the National Election Studies (NES), were carried out by the University of Michigan beginning in the late 1940s. What these studies showed was that Americans fall into three categories with regard to their political knowledge. A tiny percentage know a lot about politics, up to 50 or 60 percent know enough to answer very simple questions, and the rest know next to nothing. Surveys by the Roper organization and others confirmed the NES findings.

Contrary to expectations, by many measures the surveys showed the level of ignorance remaining constant over time. In the 1990s political scientists Michael X. Delli Carpini and Scott Keeter, reviewing thousands of questions from three groups of surveys over four decades, concluded that there was statistically little difference among the knowledge levels of the parents of the Silent Generation of the 1950s, the parents of the Baby Boomers of the 1960s, and American parents today. (By some measures, as we'll see, Americans are dumber today than their parents of a generation ago.)

Some of the numbers are hard to fathom in a country where, for at least a century, all children have been required by law to attend grade school or be home-schooled. One would expect people, even those who do not closely follow the news, to be able to answer basic civics questions—but, in fact, only a small minority can. In 1950, at a time when the Democrats and Republicans were working out a bipartisan approach to foreign affairs, Americans were asked what a bipartisan foreign policy was. Only 26 percent could do so. In 1952, just 27 percent of adults could name two branches of government. In 1955, when the Foreign Service was constantly in the news after Senator Joe McCarthy leveled charges that it was filled with communists, just 19 percent were able to explain what the Foreign Service was. The same year, just 35 percent were able to define the term *Electoral College*.

Skipping ahead a generation: In 1978 Americans were asked how many years a member of the House of Representatives served between elections. Just 30 percent correctly answered two years. Asked around the same time to name a single UN agency, just 35 percent could do so. In 1986 only 30 percent knew that *Roe v. Wade* was the

Supreme Court decision that ruled abortion legal more than a decade earlier. In 1991 Americans were asked how long the term of a U.S. senator is. Just 25 percent correctly answered six years. How many senators are there? A poll a few years ago found that only 20 percent know that there are 100 senators, though the latter number has remained constant for the last half-century (and is easy to remember). Encouragingly, today the proportion of Americans who can correctly identify and name the three branches of government is up to 40 percent, but that number is still below a majority.

Polls over the past three decades measuring Americans' knowledge of history show similarly dismal results. What happened in 1066? Just 10 percent know it is the date of the Norman Conquest. Who said the "world must be made safe for democracy"? Just 14 percent know it was Woodrow Wilson. Who was Plato? Just 34 percent know. Which country dropped the nuclear bomb? A majority of Americans do not know that it is their own country that is the only one to have used nuclear weapons. Who killed John F. Kennedy? Some 70 percent, influenced by popular movies such as Oliver Stone's *JFK*, buy the crackpot conspiracy theories. Who was America's greatest president? According to a Gallup poll in 2005, a majority answered that it was a president from the last half-century: 20 percent said Reagan, 15 percent Bill Clinton, 12 percent John Kennedy, 5 percent George W. Bush. Only 14 percent picked Lincoln and only 5 percent picked Washington. And the worst president? For years Americans would include in the list Herbert Hoover. But no more. Most today do not know who Herbert Hoover was, according to the University of Pennsylvania's National Annenberg Election Survey in 2004. Just 43 percent could correctly identify him.

The only history questions a majority of Americans can answer correctly are the most basic ones. What happened at Pearl Harbor? A great majority know: 84 percent. Who followed JFK in the White House? "LBJ," answer 83 percent. What was the Holocaust? Nearly 70 percent know. (Thirty percent don't?) But it comes as something of a shock that in 1983 just 81 percent knew who Lee Harvey Oswald was and that in 1985 only 81 percent could identify Martin Luther King, Jr.

Who these poor souls were who didn't recognize Martin Luther King's name we cannot know for sure. Research suggests that they were probably impoverished (the poor tend to know less on the whole about politics and history than others) or simply unschooled, categories that usually overlap. But even Americans in the middle class who attend college exhibit profound ignorance. A report in 2007 published by the Intercollegiate Studies Institute found that, on average, 14,000 randomly selected college students at fifty schools around the country scored under 55 (out of 100) on a test that measured knowledge of basic American civics. Fewer than half knew that Yorktown was the last battle of the American Revolution. Surprisingly, seniors often tested lower than freshmen (the explanation was apparently that many students by their senior year had forgotten what they learned in high school). An experience I had a decade or so ago, aboard a train heading from Paris to Amsterdam, suggests the dimensions of the problem. I had a conversation with a young American who had graduated from college and was now considering medical school. He had received good grades in school. He was articulate. And he was anything but poor, as was clear from the fact that he was spending the summer tooling around Europe. But when the subject involved history, he was stumped. When the conversation turned to Joseph Stalin he had to ask who Stalin was. What else, I wondered, did he not know if he didn't know this?

The optimists point to surveys indicating that about half the country can describe some differences between the Republican and Democratic parties. But if they do not know the difference between liberals and conservatives, as surveys indicate, how can they possibly say in any meaningful way how the parties differ? And how encouraging is a statistic indicating that about half of Americans know so little about politics that they cannot tell the difference between the two main parties? The parties bear some of the blame for this sorry statistic. If they did not reinvent themselves every four years, maybe the voters would have a better idea where they stand. Still, one comes back to the question of the voters' ignorance. Again I ask the question: If they do not know this, what else do they not know?

Plenty, it turns out. Even though they are awash in news, Americans generally do not seem to absorb what it is that they are reading and hearing and watching. In 1986 one of the biggest stories of the year was Ronald Reagan's summit meeting with Mikhail Gorbachev at Geneva. This was Reagan's first meeting with a Soviet leader and it attracted enormous attention. The eyes of the world were on Geneva—and so were the eyes of America's television cameras. Interest in Gorbachev, who had been selected party chairman just seven months earlier, was intense. He was young, articulate, and charismatic—a far cry from the somnolent leaders who had led the USSR for the previous generation. Still, after the summit an ABC News/*Washington Post* poll indicated that a majority of Americans could not identify Gorbachev by name. Today fewer know the name of the recent president of Russia, Vladimir Putin.

Americans cannot even name the leaders of their own government. Sandra Day O'Connor was the first woman appointed to the U.S. Supreme Court. Fewer than half of Americans could tell you her name during the length of her entire tenure. William Rehnquist was chief justice of the Supreme Court. Just 40 percent of Americans ever knew *his* name (and only 30 percent could tell you that he was a conservative). As the country headed into the Gulf War, just 15 percent could identify Colin Powell, then chairman of the Joint Chiefs of Staff, or Dick Cheney, then secretary of defense. In 2007, the fifth year of the

Iraq War, only 21 percent could name the secretary of defense, Robert Gates. Most Americans cannot name their own member of Congress or their senators.

If the problem were simply that Americans are bad at names, one would not have to worry too much. But they do not understand the mechanics of government either. Only 34 percent know that it is the Congress that declares war (which may explain why they are not alarmed when presidents take us into wars without explicit declarations of war from the legislature). Only 35 percent know that Congress can override a presidential veto. Some 49 percent think the president can suspend the Constitution. Some 60 percent believe that he can appoint judges to the federal courts without the approval of the Senate. Some 45 percent believe that revolutionary speech is punishable under the Constitution.

On the basis of their comprehensive approach, Delli Carpini and Keeter concluded that only 5 percent of Americans could correctly answer three-fourths of the questions asked about economics; only 11 percent, the questions about domestic issues; 14 percent, the questions about foreign affairs; and 10 percent, the questions about geography. The highest score? More Americans knew the correct answers to history questions than to other kinds of questions (which will come as a surprise to many history teachers). Still, only 25 percent knew the correct answers to three-quarters of the history questions, which were rudimentary.

In 2003 the Strategic Task Force on Education Abroad investigated Americans' knowledge of world affairs. The task force concluded: "America's ignorance of the outside world" is so great as to constitute a threat to national security.

At least, you may think to yourself, we are not getting any dumber. But by some measures we are. Thomas Patterson, the director of a large recent survey known as the Vanishing Voter Project, notes that voters today are far less able than voters of yesterday to say what the political parties stand for:

> When Angus Campbell and his colleagues at the University of Michigan interviewed eligible voters in 1952 for the National Election Studies (NES) survey, they found that respondents had no difficulty saying what they liked and disliked about the Republican and Democratic parties. Only 10 percent had nothing to say about either. The Democrats were the party of "workers" and "common people," of "big government" and "regulation," and of "social security" and "jobs." Conversely, the GOP was the party of "big business" and the "well-to-do," of "small government" and "free markets," and of "low taxes" and "self-reliance."
>
> Two decades later, many respondents were left speechless when asked the same survey questions. Twenty-seven percent could say nothing about either party, a threefold increase from 1952. Only 54 percent in the 1972 NES

survey commented about both parties. Since then Americans' ability to talk about the parties has not improved substantially. There was even a time in the 1980s when more than half had no comment about one or both parties.

Actually, the situation is even worse than these statistics indicate. Young people by many measures know less today than young people forty years ago. And their news habits are worse. Newspaper reading went out in the 1960s along with the Hula Hoop. Just 20 percent of young Americans between the ages of 18 and 34 read a daily paper. And saying that isn't saying much. There's no way of knowing what part of the paper they're reading. It is likelier to encompass the comics and a quick glance at the front page than dense stories about Somalia or the budget. They aren't watching the cable news shows either. The average age of CNN's audience is 60. And they surely are not watching the network news shows, which attract mainly the Depends generation. Nor are they using the Internet in large numbers to surf for news. Only 11 percent say that they regularly click on news web pages. (Yes, many young people watch Jon Stewart's *The Daily Show*. A survey in 2007 by the Pew Research Center found that 54 percent of the viewers of *The Daily Show* score in the "high knowledge" news category— about the same as the viewers of the *O'Reilly Factor* on Fox News.)

Compared with Americans generally—and this isn't saying much either, given *their* low level of interest in the news—young people are the least informed of any age cohort save possibly for those confined to nursing homes. In fact, the young are so indifferent to newspapers that they single-handedly are responsible for the dismally low newspaper readership rates that are bandied about. Excluding the young, some 70 percent of Americans read a newspaper daily. It's the young who bring the average down to 50 percent or so.

In earlier generations—the 1950s, for example—young people read newspapers and digested the news at rates similar to those of the general population. Nothing indicates that the current generation of young people will suddenly begin following the news when they turn 35 or 40. Indeed, a half-century of studies suggest that most people who do not pick up the news habit in their 20s probably never will.

Young people today find the news irrelevant. When one college teacher required a class to listen to NPR for an hour, one student summed up the general reaction to the experience by calling it "torture." Bored by politics, students shun the rituals of civic life, voting in lower numbers than other Americans (though a small uptick in civic participation became apparent in recent surveys). U.S. Census data indicate that voters aged 18 to 24 turn out in low numbers. In 1972, when 18-year-olds got the vote, 52 percent cast a ballot. In subsequent years far fewer voted: from 1976–1984, 43 percent; in 1988, 40 percent; in 1992, 50 percent; in 1996, 35 percent; in 2000, 36 percent. In 2004, despite the most intense get-out-the-vote effort ever focused on young people, just 47 percent took the time to cast a ballot. The University of Maryland's Center for Information & Research on Civic Learning & Engagement, which crunched the numbers, found the increase gratifying. But since when is a 47 percent turnout cause for celebration? And as the Center conceded, 2004 may just have been a temporary blip. Turnout in the same age group increased in 1992 too, owing to Ross Perot's exciting campaign and Bill Clinton's own youthfulness—and then declined precipitously during the following election, as indicated above.

Since young people on the whole scarcely follow politics, one may wish to consider whether we even want them to vote. Asked in 2000 to identify the presidential candidate who was the chief sponsor of Campaign Finance Reform—Senator John McCain—just 4 percent of people between the ages of 18 and 24 could do so. As the primary season began in February, fewer than half in the same age group knew that George W. Bush was even a candidate. Only 12 percent knew that McCain was also a candidate, even though he was said to be especially appealing to young people.

One news subject in recent history did attract the interest of the young: 9/11. A poll by Pew at the end of 2001 found that 61 percent of adult Americans under age

30 said that they were following the story closely. But few found any other news subjects compelling that year. Anthrax? Just 32 percent indicated it was important enough to follow. The economy? Again, just 32 percent. The capture of Kabul? Just 20 percent. The debate about federalizing airport security? 21 percent.

It would appear that young people today are doing very little reading of any kind whatsoever. In 2004 the National Endowment for the Arts, consulting a vast array of surveys including the U.S. Census, found that just 43 percent of young people ages 18 to 24 read literature. In 1982 the number was 60 percent. A majority also do not read newspapers, fiction, poetry, or drama. Save for the possibility that they are reading the Bible or works of non-fiction, for which solid statistics are unavailable, it would appear that this generation is less well read than any other since statistics began to be kept.

The studies demonstrating that young people know less today than young people a generation ago do not get much publicity. What one hears about are the pioneer steps the young are taking politically. Headlines from the 2004 presidential election featured numerous stories about young people who were following the campaign on blogs, then a new phenomenon. Other stories focused on the help that young Deaniacs gave Howard Dean by arranging to raise funds through innovative Internet appeals. Still other stories reported that the Deaniacs were networking all over the country through the Internet website meetup.com.

One did not hear that we have raised another Silent Generation. But have we not? The statistics about young people today are fairly clear: As a group they do not vote in large numbers, most do not read newspapers, and most do not follow the news. (Barack Obama has recently inspired greater participation, but at this stage it is too early to tell if the effect will be lasting.)

A few years ago, when I began teaching journalism at a large university in the Washington D.C. area, I discovered to my amazement that even journalism students in graduate school in the nation's capital did not share my enthusiasm for news. This was a good school and these were good students. They were intelligent and they were motivated. Most were in their late 20s or early 30s. But only two or three out of a class of twenty or so read either the *Washington Post* or the *New York Times* daily. To get them to read the paper I had to insist on their taking weekly current events quizzes. If journalism students like these did not want to read the major papers, how likely was it that average Americans without a career stake in the news would want to?

Millions every year are now spent on the effort to answer the question: What do the voters want? The honest answer would be that often they themselves do not really know because they do not know enough to say. Few, however, admit this.

In the election of 2004 one of the hot issues was gay marriage. But gauging public opinion on the subject was difficult. Asked in one national poll whether they supported a constitutional amendment allowing only marriages between a man and a woman, a majority said yes. But three questions later a majority also agreed that "defining marriage was not an important enough issue to be worth changing the Constitution." The *New York Times* wryly summed up the results: Americans clearly favor amending the Constitution but not changing it.

Just before the election of 2000 the Vanishing Voter Project asked voters to identify the policy positions that George W. Bush and Al Gore had taken on twelve critical issues. Six of the questions concerned Bush's position on issues, six Gore's. Some questions were easy.

QUESTION: Do you happen to know whether Bush favors or opposes a large cut in personal income taxes?

QUESTION: Do you happen to know whether Gore favors or opposes expanding Medicare for retirees to cover the costs of prescription drugs?

Others were more difficult, though the issues had been bandied about during the campaign since the Iowa caucuses in January, ten months earlier.

QUESTION: Do you happen to know whether Bush favors or opposes a ban on very large contributions to political candidates?

Question: Do you happen to know whether Gore favors or opposes allowing workers to invest a portion of their payroll taxes in private retirement accounts rather than having all of it go toward social security?

According to project director Thomas Patterson, a majority of voters could correctly identify the candidate's position on only two issues. "On all other issues," he reported, "less than half could correctly identify the candidates' positions, and many guessed wrong." To the question about Bush's position on campaign contributions, just one in ten correctly answered that he opposed a ban.

Does it matter if people are ignorant?

There are many subjects about which the ordinary voter need know nothing. The conscientious citizen has no obligation to plow through the federal budget, for example. One suspects there are not many politicians themselves who have bothered to do so. Nor do voters have an obligation to read the laws passed in their name. We do expect members of Congress to read the bills they are asked to vote on, but we know from experience that often they do not, either having failed to take the time to do so or having been denied the opportunity to do so by their leaders, who for one reason or another often rush bills through. Reading the text of laws is, in any case, often unhelpful. The chairpersons in charge of drafting them often include provisions only a detective could untangle.

The U.S. code is rife with clauses like this: *The Congress hereby appropriates X dollars for the purchase of 500 widgets that measure 3 inches by 4 inches by 2 inches from any company incorporated on October 20, 1965, in Any City USA situated in block 10 of district 3.* Of course, only one company fits the description. Upon investigation it turns out to be owned by the chairperson's biggest contributor. That is more than any citizens acting on their own could possibly divine. It is not essential that the voter know every single way in which the U.S. code is manipulated to benefit special interests. All that is required is that the voter know that rigging of the U.S. code in favor of certain interests is probably common. The media are perfectly capable of communicating this message. Voters are perfectly capable of absorbing it. Armed with this knowledge, the voter knows to be wary of claims that the U.S. code treats one and all alike with fairness.

There are, however, innumerable subjects about which a general knowledge is insufficient. In these cases, ignorance of the details is more than a minor problem. An appalling ignorance of Social Security, to take just one example, has left Americans unable to see how their money has been spent, whether the system is viable, and what measures are needed to shore it up.

How many know that the system is running a surplus? And that this surplus—some $150 *billion* a year—is actually quite substantial, even by Washington standards? And how many know that the system has been in surplus since 1983?

Few, of course. Ignorance of the facts has led to a fundamentally dishonest debate about Social Security.

During all the years the surpluses were building, the Democrats in Congress pretended the money was theirs to be spent as if it were the same as all the other tax dollars collected by the government. And spend it they did whenever they had the chance, with no hint that they were perhaps disbursing funds that actually should be held in reserve for later use. (Social Security taxes were expressly raised in 1983 in order to build up the system's funds when bankruptcy had loomed.) Not until the rest of the budget was in surplus (in 1999) did it suddenly occur to them that the money should be saved. And it appears that the only reason they felt compelled at this point to acknowledge that the money was needed for Social Security was that they wanted to blunt the Republicans' call for tax cuts. The Social Security surplus could not be used to pay both for the large tax cuts Republicans wanted and for the future retirement benefits of aging Boomers.

The Republicans have been equally unctuous. While they have claimed that they are terribly worried about Social Security they have been busy irresponsibly spending the system's surplus on tax cuts, one cut after another. First Reagan used the surplus to hide the impact of *his* tax cuts and then George W. Bush used it to hide the impact of *his* cuts. Neither ever acknowledged that it was precisely the surplus in Social Security's accounts that made it even plausible for them to cut taxes. Take those Bush tax cuts. Bush claimed the cuts were made possible by several years of past surpluses and the prospect of even more years of surpluses. But subtracting from the federal budget the overflow funds generated by Social Security, we find that the government ran a surplus for just two years during the period the national debt was declining: 1999 and 2000. In the other years when the government ran a surplus, 1998 and 2001, it was because of Social Security and only because of Social Security. That is, the putative surpluses of 1998 and 2001, which Mr. Bush cited in defense of his tax cuts, were in reality pure fiction. Without Social Security the government would have been in debt those two years. And yet in 2001 President Bush told the country that tax cuts were not only needed but affordable because of our splendid surplus.

Today conservatives argue that the Social Security Trust Fund is a fiction. They are correct. The money was spent. They helped spend it.

To this debate about Social Security—which, once one understands what has been happening, is actually quite absorbing—the public has largely responded with indifference. A surprising 2001 Pew study found that just 19 percent of Americans understand that the United States ever ran a surplus at all, however defined, in the 1990s or 2000s. And only 50 percent of Americans, according to an Annenberg study in 2004, understand that President Bush favors privatizing Social Security. Polls indicate that people are scared that the system is going bust, no doubt

thanks in part to Mr. Bush's doom-and-gloom prognosti-
cations. But they haven't the faintest idea what going bust
means. And in fact, the system can be kept going without
fundamental change simply by raising the cap on taxed income and pushing back the retirement age a few years.

How much ignorance can a country stand? There have
to be terrible consequences when it reaches a certain
level. But what level? And with what consequences, exactly? The answers to these questions are unknowable.
But can we doubt that, if we persist along the path we are
on, we shall one day, perhaps not too far into the distant
future, find out the answers?

3

Are the Voters Irrational?

◆

A supporter once called out, "Governor Stevenson, all
thinking people are for you!" And Adlai Stevenson answered, "That's not enough. I need a majority."
— Scott Simon

One of the questions political scientists faced after uncov-
ering the evidence of ignorance we have just reviewed is
whether voters find ways to compensate for their knowledge deficit. If they do, then it could be argued that
(1) things aren't so bad and (2) the voters are rational.

So what did the political scientists discover? To their
delight they found that voters have invented a variety of
methods to make up, in part, for their ignorance. Even
inattentive voters glean much of what they need to know
to cast a ballot intelligently through various "shortcuts."
A voter, for example, may decide that he should vote for
Candidate X because his local newspaper endorsed X and

he generally agrees with the positions the paper takes. Or a voter may simply decide that he generally agrees with the Democrats and therefore votes for Democrats. Parties are like brands; people learn over time which to trust and not trust. Or a voter may follow the advice of a well-informed friend who shares his views. We all use such shortcuts, known as heuristics, so the fact that some voters rely on them is reassuring. In Seattle, where I live, judges are elected. It is impossible to know enough about all but a handful of these judges even if one is a scrupulously attentive voter. So when the day comes to vote, I use heuristics to decide. I turn to a local free paper I trust, the *Seattle Weekly*, to see whom the editors are backing. Unless I have independent knowledge about one of the judges, I follow the paper's advice.

The consensus in the political science profession is that voters are rational. And there are many reasons for thinking that they are. One is that they appear able to distinguish between problems a president can do something about and those he cannot. When crime was a big issue a few years ago they realized that the problem primarily had to be addressed at the local level, even though they liked candidates to talk about the subject. Most voters understand that the two main parties are different, and many (though probably not a majority) get one of the most critical ways in which they are different: that Democrats are more concerned with unemployment and that Republicans are more concerned with inflation. But they do not grasp the reason for the difference: that Democrats are less likely to tackle inflation because of the risk that tight money policies may reduce employment.

Yet another sign of the voter's intelligence is that celebrity status, while important, is not always decisive. In 1980 Democratic voters inclined to support Senator Ted Kennedy's challenge to President Jimmy Carter changed their minds the more they watched Kennedy campaign. That is, they actually watched the news, picked up information about the campaign, and based their opinion on hard evidence. In 1984 Democrats were excited about the candidacy of Senator John Glenn, who had won fame as the first American to orbit the earth. But they watched enough news shows to gather that he was a lackluster campaigner and turned to other candidates. Celebrity, in other words, only gives a candidate the chance to be taken seriously by the electorate. It does not guarantee victory.

While voters do not follow the campaigns closely enough to be able to say where the candidates stand on a variety of issues, they often pay close attention to the one or two issues they really care about. In 1980 the Republican presidential contest turned on the performance of Ronald Reagan and George H. W. Bush at a famous debate in Nashua, New Hampshire. When the moderator turned off the sound system, Reagan, borrowing a line Spencer Tracy used in the movie *State of the Union*, shot back, "I paid for this microphone, Mr. Green!" The crowd was electrified. But when the election was held, voters in favor of the Equal Rights Amendment stayed with Bush because he shared their views and Reagan did not. Four years later, polls showed that Democratic voters concerned about the corruption of unions deserted Walter Mondale as his support for unions became known. In other words: In these two elections, issues counted. Voters watched the news and they absorbed it.

The ability of voters to watch out for their own interests is one of the critical pieces of evidence that they are rational. Thus, the elderly tend to follow news about Social Security closely, and even the poor, who ordinarily are less likely than others to score high on political knowledge tests, know a lot about welfare. They know which politicians support welfare and how the system works. Farmers, likewise, are attentive to debates about farm policy. In one of the first cases of political rationality documented by researchers, seven out of ten Democrats disillusioned with FDR's farm policy after the 1936 election switched to the Republican Wendell Wilkie in 1940.

It is often said that elections are referendums on the past. One of the reasons for this is that voters tend to punish politicians when they do something the voters disapprove of, as FDR discovered when those farmers deserted him. In these cases politics is highly rational.

Voters also punish failure—as Herbert Hoover discovered in 1932. Voters may not be able to tell you why a politician failed. When the economy turns south, few voters can assess the president's responsibility for unfavorable conditions. But they usually know when conditions are bad and they hold those in office at the time responsible. "Throw the bums out" may not be a sophisticated response to adversity but it is a rational one.

Political consultants know that the hardest thing to do is to change a voter's mind once an impression has taken hold. But people do change their minds on occasion when information is packaged well. A textbook example of this scenario took place at the 1992 Democratic Convention. Before the convention voters tended to think that Bill Clinton was a child of privilege, probably because they had heard he went to Yale University. To correct this misimpression his handlers broadcast a short movie, *The Man from Hope*, made by the slick Hollywood producers who had the hit TV show *Designing Women*. Polling at the end of the convention showed that voters now believed that Clinton was a man of modest means who had risen by his own efforts.

Voters are also known to engage in what is called "strategic voting." In 2006, for example, voters in Rhode Island threw out the incumbent senator, Lincoln Chafee, despite high personal approval ratings. Why? Because he was a Republican. Voters knew he was a Republican and understood the significance of voting for a Republican with a closely divided Senate. Rather than risk shifting control of the Senate to the Republicans, they voted against Chafee, a man with a storied last name in Rhode Island politics (his father had served as both governor and senator), in favor of a Democrat they had never heard of before. Whether one agrees with their judgment or not, it is obvious that they were paying attention to national political developments.

Voters often pay enough attention to know that voting for a particular candidate can "send a message." In 1968 millions voted for George Wallace to send a message to the country about their dissatisfaction with the two major parties. Twenty years later voters cast ballots for Jesse Jackson to signal their support for a black presidential candidate who offered a decidedly left-wing approach to politics. Both times, voters knew that their candidates did not have a chance of winning. But they also knew that voting for them was not the same as throwing away their vote. They got the difference. Voters are usually chary of throwing away their votes on a loser. In 2004 voters in New Hampshire watched Howard Dean's meltdown in Iowa and abandoned him. Dean, who had been ahead of John Kerry by 30 percent, ended up a week later coming in second. Shortly thereafter Dean dropped out of the race. Once again voters had absorbed information (in this case, the primary results in Iowa) and acted on it.

This is the positive part of the story political scientists tell. Now for the rest. As the reader has no doubt already surmised, it's grim.

Let's begin with the American voter's opinion of the Public Affairs Act of 1975. One poll shows that 40 percent of Americans hold an opinion about it. The trouble with this is that there is no such law. Pollsters made it up to find out if people guess at the questions they are given. Apparently, the answer is: yes.

The mistakes voters make fall into four basic patterns, according to Samuel Popkin's review of the evidence. The first mistake is what is known as the Drunkard's Search. Like the drunk who looks for his lost keys under a sidewalk lamp because "that's where the best light is," voters tend to pick up information passively. The second mistake is that voters tend to remember personal information about candidates rather than hard facts about issues. Personal information picked up later tends to block out facts about issues learned earlier. Third, voters have a preference for yes/no answers, which provide "pseudo-certainty." They do not like ambiguity and they abhor complexity. Fourth, voters do not see the connections between actions and results. If the economy improves during a president's term, voters tend to give him the credit without knowing what, if anything, the president did or did not do to bring about these favorable conditions.

Again and again what the polls show is that Americans cannot make up for their lack of basic knowledge even if they shrewdly employ shortcuts. If shortcuts were a good substitute, what happened in 2003 and 2004 when the voters were misled about 9/11, Saddam, and al Qaeda would not have happened.

Remember the Nashua debate that political scientists point to as evidence of the voter's rationality? Reagan

stole the show with his quick retort about the microphone, but his great moment was a triumph only because
the voters based their assessment of the event solely on
what they saw and heard and not on the circumstances.
Reagan, who had been lagging in the polls, had invited
George H.W. Bush, the leader with "Big Mo" after a victory in the Iowa caucuses, to participate in a one-on-one
debate. Then Reagan secretly invited the other candidates
to attend, calculating that they would use their time to
criticize Bush, with himself the beneficiary. But when
Bush showed up and found the other candidates expecting
to go on stage, he became upset at what he considered a
cheap trick, and insisted the others leave. The moderator
agreed with him. It was at that moment that Reagan
pounced, leaving the impression to those who didn't
know the full story that he was fighting on behalf of fairness and inclusiveness when in fact his true motive was to
sandbag Bush. Because Bush did not immediately explain
what was happening, the voters came away thinking that
he was the villain, a man afraid to debate his rivals. This
episode tells us lots about Bush, particularly his inferiority
as an actor, but it doesn't say much for the voters except
that they enjoy a good show and a politician with a flair
for drama.

Or take Bush's "read my lips" pledge not to raise taxes.
Political scientists regard the fierce reaction to his decision to break his pledge as evidence that voters had been
paying attention to what he said in 1988 and that they

remembered what he said. But in a rational world Bush never would have made his pledge in the first place. Not only could he not fairly anticipate changing conditions that might require a tax increase, but it was obvious at the time that the Reagan deficits had become so extreme that a tax increase of a substantial size would be needed to bring in more revenue. Truly rational voters would have greeted Bush's decision to break his pledge with a shrug, recognizing that his anti-tax promise was simply campaign rhetoric. Bush himself believed that was all it was. When the firestorm broke he was caught off-guard. He had not taken his campaign rhetoric seriously and was surprised that the voters had. In a rational world they wouldn't have.

Particularly difficult for voters is following debates about issues. Issues often require knowledge the voters lack. In the absence of knowledge irrational biases often dictate the policies voters support. Take economics. According to Bryan Caplan, the public is irrationally biased in four different ways against good public policies broadly supported by economists. First, the public, fearful of the greed of the selfish, generally is suspicious of markets. Second, the public has an anti-foreign bias. That is, people generally underestimate the benefit of foreign trade. Third, the public is fixated on employment as a measure of economic success; economists, in contrast, focus on productivity. Fourth, the public tends to believe things are getting worse, not better; unlike economists who seek to see the big picture, voters tend toward pessimism, seizing on bits of bad economic news. Given the biases of the public, politicians who possess a solid grasp of economics have to either conceal their real views through smoke-and-mirror games or outright lie about what they actually believe. In office they may well follow sound policies, but they may not. One thinks of Richard Nixon's hypocritical embrace of wage and price controls, which helped aggravate the inflationary pressures the policy was designed to mitigate by creating an artificial market. When the controls finally were lifted, prices exploded.

The best reason we have for thinking that the voters are irrational is that our politics are. If the voters were rational our politics would be rational. They aren't.

During the long, drawn-out soap opera involving Monica Lewinsky, both sides in the drama played on the public's irrationality. Right-wingers counted on the public's interest in finding out the most intimate details of their president's sex life. Kenneth Starr's report to the Congress was full of salacious material calculated to appeal to people's emotions. For his part, Bill Clinton continually bet that he could bamboozle people. Having convinced millions in 1992 he was innocent of an affair with Gennifer Flowers—despite audiotapes on which he could be heard coaching her on how to mislead reporters—he once again commenced to persuade voters that he was innocent of an affair with Lewinsky. A calm review of the evidence at the time would have suggested the implausibility of his case, even knowing he was the victim of a right-wing conspiracy—as his wife Hillary correctly asserted. His claim, for instance, of repeatedly calling Lewinsky on the phone so he could counsel her surely did not make sense. His attempt to find her a job sounded like the act of someone who had something to hide. But not until the stained blue dress turned up did the voters finally reach the conclusion that they had been lied to. (It is worth noting that Secretary of State Madeleine Albright and other officials in Clinton's own government were similarly taken in by his lies. Were these individuals irrational? Hardly. But ironically the ordinary voter was actually in a better position to recognize Clinton's lying for what it was than they were. Why? Washington operates on the assumption that officials may lie to the country from time to time but not to each other. Clinton broke this unspoken rule, to the surprise of his subordinates.)

The public's decision to support Clinton once it knew for a fact that he had lied is evidence of a degree of rationality. Despite its disappointment in him, it remained rational enough to understand that he did not deserve to be impeached for his offenses. It also wisely understood that his enemies had overreached. The story that emerges from the Lewinsky drama is therefore mixed.

The same cannot be said for the story of the George W. Bush administration. Except for the attack on Afghanistan, it is hard to think of a major initiative he handled well. (And even Afghanistan was less than a sterling success, as

Osama bin Laden was allowed to escape from Tora Bora.)
But the populace seemed not to notice for years. Fearful of
another 9/11 attack, they hardly seemed to notice anything he did as long as he appeared to keep them safe.
While it was rational for voters to focus on safety, it was irrational to fail to ask questions. And yet that is the clear
record of what happened for five full years. When Bush
decided early on in his administration to hold fewer news
conferences than any other modern president, the public
did not protest. Nor did people seem to notice or care that
when he did subject himself to questioning it was usually
at staged events featuring groups of sympathetic voters
from his own party. Nor did the people catch on that he
used the gay-marriage issue to divide the country and rally
his political base even as he insisted his goal "as a uniter
not a divider" was to unite the country and get past the
culture war. Nor did they figure out the most basic facts
about his tax cuts: that most went to the wealthy, that the
abolition of the estate tax benefited the richest 1 percent of
taxpayers rather than the family farmer or small businessman as claimed, that tax cuts seemed to be the all-purpose
cure whether times were good (as in 2000) or bad (as in
2001). When Bush claimed that he did not care about the
polls, people believed him, even though we know for a fact
that both he and his chief political advisor, Karl Rove,
studied the polls.

Bush's assertion after the 9/11 attack that our enemies
hated us because we are free was mindless—but people be-

lieved it. His claim that oil had nothing to do with our invasion of Iraq was downright comical—but a majority of people believed it. And then of course there was the granddaddy of all misinformation, the dropped hint that Saddam Hussein was somehow in league with the people who attacked us on 9/11—and the American public believed that, too, even after the president was pressured by the media to declare before the cameras in a terse statement that there was no evidence linking Saddam and 9/11.

After repeatedly conning people Bush seemed to become convinced that he could say or do anything and get away with it. But in the fall of 2005 he finally discovered that there were limits when he nominated Harriet Miers, who had never served as a judge, as his second Supreme Court pick. Significantly, it wasn't ordinary voters who rebelled when he described her as one of the most experienced lawyers in the country and, laughably, the best qualified for the position. It was his base.

The general public did express strong disapproval of his administration when an obscure government council approved a deal giving Dubai control of six American ports. To a people still traumatized by 9/11, in part because Bush had played on their fears repeatedly, this proposal on its face seemed harebrained (whether it was or not). But that was the only time he was reprimanded by the public in his first five years in office.

V. O. Key, Jr., one of the first political scientists to grapple with the evidence of ignorance and irrationality that turned up in surveys, argued that the voters aren't fools. But he was writing back in the 1960s. It is not clear that he would express the same confidence in the voters today, given that they often know less than their earlier counterparts. Further, anyone who reads a newspaper knows that voters today often oversimplify politics and let superficial factors affect how they vote and what they think. Especially in the television age, as we will see later, how an individual comes across can be a key determinant of his or her success or failure in politics. One need not be handsome or pretty. But a pleasing personality is an enormous asset. Candidates who lack this asset, as Richard Nixon did, often have to compensate by making raw emotional appeals to rally support. They have to fight dirty and employ fear. One of the reasons Ronald Reagan rarely resorted to blatant fear-mongering was that as a personable politician he didn't have to. People simply liked him. Irrational? Not quite. Leaders need followers, and one of the ways they attract followers in the television age is by offering us a pleasing personality. What would be irrational is voters embracing ogres. Voters aren't computers and shouldn't be considered inferior because they aren't.

There is little danger of the voters acting too much like computers, however. The problem is that they often do not act enough like computers. That is, they often do not take in enough information to make a rational calculation of their interests. Often they simply give in to their emotions.

Politicians count on their doing this. One of Reagan's keen insights was that he could cut taxes drastically without worrying that the voters would punish him for running large deficits. As long as he didn't try to make up for the loss in revenue by cutting the programs of the middle class the voters stood by him. In the election of 1984 the Democratic candidate, Walter Mondale, tried to make an issue of the budget deficit. He got nowhere. In his speech accepting his party's nomination Mondale told voters the truth, that both he and Reagan would have to raise taxes because the deficits had grown too large to be sustained without damage to the economy: "He won't tell you. I just did."

The response to Mondale's act of candor? Initially, the polls indicated that his straight talk went over well with voters. But then the Republicans began attacking Mondale and within weeks public opinion shifted. Although Mondale had the facts on his side, the voters preferred Reagan's rosy talk of Morning in America. What about those deficits? Reagan, as Mondale had predicted, grudgingly had to go along with several tax increases. These still weren't enough. By 1990 the deficit had become such a monster that Reagan's successor, George H. W. Bush, felt compelled to approve what was up to that point the largest tax increase in history. His reward for finally tackling a problem Reagan had largely sidestepped? His own party revolted, contributing to his loss two years later to Bill Clinton.

Years after the 1984 election I saw Mondale on television. The interviewer wanted to know if he still thought it was a good idea to have admitted he would raise taxes. Why yes, he stammered defensively. His interlocutor could barely keep his jaw from dropping. Mondale still didn't get it! The voters do not want the truth.*

What do they want? Myths.

---

*I should note that Mondale's act of candor in 1984 was an act of political expediency that backfired. Pundits had criticized Mondale for pandering. By taking a strong stand in favor of a tax increase he hoped to blunt such talk.

4

The Importance of Myths

◆

If the people believe there's an imaginary river out
there, you don't tell them there's no river there. You
build an imaginary bridge over the imaginary river.

—Nikita S. Khrushchev
(as remembered by Richard Nixon)

Myths have played a role in our politics from the beginning. Holding us together as a people in the early years of
the Republic like a kind of national glue was the myth of
George Washington. In a country with weak national institutions and no traditions, the Washington myth was
vital. Had he not been godlike we still would have pretended that he was. Between the Revolution and the Civil
War we went on a mythmaking binge, turning almost
everybody who came to prominence into a larger-than-
life mythical character: Ben Franklin, Davy Crockett, Abe

Lincoln, and dozens of others. We told stories about them to each other and to our children. We didn't call it nation-building, but that was what we were doing. We were trying to define ourselves and our values through myths. Myths were especially important to us because as a nation of immigrants we lacked a common ancestry and tribal ties. All that we really had in common were those myths.

Given the prominence of myths even in the 1790s and early 1800s, when our politics remained under the control of a small elite of white male property holders, it is evident that we cannot fault the masses for their susceptibility to myths. The Founding Fathers themselves fell for the myths, save possibly for the ornery John Adams, who denounced the merry mythmaking he encountered all around him as so much nonsense (in part, because he felt that his own contributions had been underestimated). But there is no denying that after the masses got the vote in the 1830s (when property qualifications were abolished), myths became the driving force in our politics. Whereas in the past politicians had debated issues in public, in detail, and often at a high level, now more and more they invoked myths. Particularly in the modern era myths have been vital because they help voters sort through the chaos of conflicting information in which they find themselves almost drowning.

Most of the objectionable aspects of politics to which I have drawn attention in this book are wholly due to the

direct involvement of the masses in elections.* Because of
the difficulty of engaging the masses in a broad and serious debate about issues, politicians began resorting to
fake imagery, slogans, songs, torchlight parades, and
bombastic rhetoric. On one occasion, partisans even
rolled a giant cheese ball to the White House in order to
attract attention and generate a kind of gee-whiz awe
among the spectators. But above all the politicians used
myths, feeding them into an all-American player piano,
out of which came what sounded like music to the ears of
the voters.

Any number of dates might be selected as a key turning point. But if one must choose, the most obvious is
1840—an election year fittingly remembered for a slogan. The winner, Whig William Henry Harrison, was
the Tippecanoe referred to in the famous line "Tippecanoe and Tyler, too." Though this election wasn't the first
to feature a slogan, the Tippecanoe line was the first
campaign slogan anybody still recalls. No one today remembers "Huzzah for Gen. Jackson! Down with the
Yankees," or "Marty Van Ruin," a deft jab at Harrison's
opponent, Martin Van Buren, on whose watch the economy had slipped into a devastating depression. But after

---

*This is not to suggest that politics in the earlier period was practiced
with perfection. Politics was just as partisan and people were just as nasty
as today, Jeffersonians attacking George Washington himself with such
ugly ripostes that Washington complained he was treated no better than a
common pickpocket.

Tippecanoe won the Executive Mansion with the help of a dazzling slogan, every elected president of the United States came into office, in part, on the back of a simplistic phrase designed to generate an emotional charge from the masses.

There wasn't much more to Harrison's election than his various slogans. He had no qualification for office other than that he was once a general. He had not written any books. He had never given a memorable speech. He had no position on the major issues of the day. The great fear of his handlers was that he might actually say something if given the chance to speak at a public gathering. Party bosses arranged that, should Harrison be elected, Daniel Webster and Henry Clay would actually run the government—Clay from his position in the Senate and Webster from his in the cabinet. When the party convened to select Harrison, the delegates even chose to forego the writing of a party platform. His chief claim, that he was a general, was overrated. He hadn't distinguished himself in battle beyond winning a much-disputed victory over Indians at the Battle of Tippecanoe nearly thirty years earlier, where he lost about a fourth of his troops. But borrowing a page from the Democrats, who had won the White House riding on the reputation of war hero Andrew Jackson, the Whigs chose to build the campaign of 1840 around Harrison. The Democrats had had their war hero and now the Whigs would have *theirs*.

The question of whether a system based on mass suf-frage could rise to the level of the old system was defini-tively answered that fall. The vacuousness of the campaign was breathtaking. One Whig poem captured the spirit perfectly:

> *Without a why or a wherefore*
> *We'll go for Harrison therefore.*

In the hopeful opening days of the campaign season the opposition thought to subject the general to withering ridicule. "Give him a barrel of hard cider, and settle a pension of two thousand a year upon him," claimed a newspaper in Baltimore, "and our word for it, he will sit the remainder of his days content in a log cabin, by the side of a 'sea-coal' fire and study moral philosophy." Un-fortunately for the Democrats the jibe backfired. The log cabin proved to be a potent symbol of down-to-earth de-mocracy if ever there was one. Thereafter it would be every politician's dream to be associated with it.

Though he claimed that he was born in a log cabin, Mr. Harrison's father, a signer of the Declaration of Indepen-dence, had seen fit to raise Harrison in a multi-story red-brick mansion, which one may still visit, located on the James River in Virginia. But no one much cared if the candidate lied. Nor did anyone seem to care that his op-ponent, Martin Van Buren, actually had been born poor and was now being falsely depicted by his enemies as something of a foppish elitist.

Poor Harrison died a month after taking office. As all trivia aficionados know, he gave the longest inaugural address in history and served the shortest term in consequence of having caught pneumonia on the day he was sworn in. But his election may be said to have been one of the most important of the nineteenth century as a commentary on American democracy. Its importance derives from the way Harrison won. Add in television commercials and several other features and you pretty much have a picture of the modern American political campaign. The use of the log cabin myth was particularly telling.

Politicians quickly learned that mass voters have little patience for facts. Myths move people, facts do not. And myths are so powerful that facts are as nothing by comparison. If one could take a Harrison, one of the members of the FFV (First Families of Virginia), and pass him off as a Representative Man, then anything is possible. All one needs is to find the right myth and stuff into it the man whom you want to sell.

Sometimes, as in the case of Lincoln, there was a good fit between man and myth. Lincoln the Rail Splitter—was there ever a more splendid mythical image than this?—had indeed split rails and been born in a log cabin. But always the myth obscured more than it revealed. By the time Lincoln became a candidate for the presidency he was a successful railroad attorney who had long since distanced himself from his frontier roots. While others romanticized his impoverished past, he most certainly did not.

Today's political consultants have begun advising candidates that what they need more than anything else is a compelling storyline. In 2004 Tom Vilsack, the obscure governor of Iowa, was briefly considered a potential candidate for the vice presidency because, according to a profile in the *New York Times*, he could be packaged as a self-made man who had begun life as an abandoned orphan. The details added to his attraction. His adoptive mother had been an abusive alcoholic with whom he subsequently reconciled. His father had lost the family fortune. One does not wish to play down the obviously valiant efforts Mr. Vilsack must have made to rise above his circumstances, but his story does sound rather Oprahish. On the other hand, given the demands of mass politics, that is hardly a disadvantage. Had Oprah featured Mr. Vilsack on her show to relate his story, it is not inconceivable that he rather than John Edwards might have ended up on the ticket with John Kerry.

Common to most of the myths told about presidents is the up-from-the-bottom, rags-to-riches theme of Vilsack's story. This is interesting as most presidents, of course, were not born poor. According to a detailed study by historian Edward Pessen, three-fourths have come from the upper-middle or upper classes. Many were downright honest-to-goodness rich folk, starting with George Washington, who was one of the richest men in America. But the misfortune of having been born into wealth has seldom been a bar to high office. It has proven amazingly simple to pass off the wealthy as common citizens.

One of the last presidents not to try was Franklin Roosevelt. He casually flaunted his wealth and inherited position. His use of a cigarette holder seemed calculated to put distance between him and the common man. And what other modern politician has dared wear a cape? Even his voice sounded upper crust. Listening to his fireside chats, one couldn't help but conclude that here was a man of good breeding. But then FDR had the story of surviving polio. That served the purpose of humanizing him for the masses. He may not have had to triumph over poverty, but it did take him a couple of years to wiggle two toes. And though the public never understood the depth of his illness and that it had robbed him permanently of the use of his legs, people perfectly understood that he had gone through a terrible ordeal. He who had once seemed brash and innocent now came across like an ordinary fellow who'd faced a crisis and met it. Just as he had beat polio, he would help the country beat the Depression.

Most other American pols have not had nearly as good a story to tell. FDR's cousin Teddy had to make do with the tale of his triumph over childhood asthma and his ride up San Juan Hill (actually, Kettle Hill). John Kennedy had to inflate the story of the sinking of his

PT 109 boat in World War II. George Herbert Walker Bush was reduced to bragging that he ate pork rinds. His son has made himself sound like a cornpone hick. John Kerry, married to one of the wealthiest women in America by virtue of her previous marriage to a member of the Heinz ketchup family, had himself photographed standing in front of a bale of hay (his wife's mansion was deliberately kept out of view). Howard Dean, who was raised in an apartment on Park Avenue, gave a speech in Iowa in which he referred to himself and his audience of farmers as "us rural people."

Lovely, eh? We may begin to think, as the satirist John Keats would say, there's more honesty in the used-car business where a Caddie's a Caddie and a heap's pretty much a heap. But setting aside for a moment our moral scruples to take in objectively the scene of the typical campaign, we can't help but admire the candidates' dexterity. It is one of the great marvels of American politics. When we consider that the rich once feared the masses' getting the right to vote, we can't help but wish that there truly were a way to travel back through time to let them know how things turned out. Wouldn't they be surprised! Americans en masse proved to have no interest in using their power at the polls to confiscate the wealth of the rich except during the period economists refer to as the Great Compression (1933–1960s), when taxes on the rich were high. What the masses mainly demand is that politicians appear ordinary—that is, human, like them.

What George W. Bush benefited from over and over again as he stumbled from one misadventure to another was the public's susceptibility to the appealing myth he had created for himself as the Hick President. He took his vacations in Crawford, Texas. He wore a big Western-style belt buckle on his waist. He bragged to Yale students that he had earned a C average. He used bad grammar. He confided that he wanted Osama bin Laden dead or alive. And at Ground Zero, with his arm casually draped over a firefighter's shoulder, he used a megaphone to declare that we would get our revenge.

Was he really dumb, or did he just pretend to be? Whole books have been produced to demonstrate that he *is* dumb. But is it not more likely that he deliberately dumbed down his message and adjusted his image to persuade the folks at home watching him on TV that he is one of them? The great danger to his career from the beginning was never that he would be perceived as dumb, but that ordinary folks would hold his elite background and education against him as voters in the nineteenth congressional district in West Texas did during his first run for office in 1978. It is truly remarkable that a man with his distinguished educational pedigree—Andover, Yale, and Harvard—and his membership in one of the country's greatest political dynasties came to be regarded as a man of the people. Previous patrician presidents like FDR and John Kennedy had persuaded people that they identified with the common man.

Bush alone succeeded in convincing people he was a common man.

This is not to say that behind President Bush's outwardly unimpressive mien there exists the brain of an intellectual giant. We know from the statements made by former Treasury Secretary Paul O'Neill and others that the president is incurious about the details of many of his administration's own policies. But some credible figures, such as the conservative *New York Times* columnist David Brooks, have attested that Mr. Bush seems a lot more knowledgeable in private than he usually does in public.

Who are *The People* with whom the politicians are so eager to identify? I use the term in this book loosely to refer to everybody minus politicians, except when I am alluding specifically to the mythologized idea of The People. But it is the myth that most people have in mind when they use the term. To them The People are a kind of red, white, and blue sprawling assemblage of ordinary, middle-class, down-to-earth, common folk. But it is best not to inquire too deeply who they really have in mind because they aren't sure. Is the local barber a member of this group? Yes, of course. The storekeeper? Sure. But what about the fellows who run the car dealership down the street and the bank on the corner of State and Main? Here's where things become complicated. You may not think that they merit inclusion, but they themselves usually do, and invariably tell pollsters that they are middle class even if they live in the biggest house in the most exclusive neighborhood in town. In short, Americans like to think of themselves as illustrious parts of The People even when their wealth and power distinguish them from ordinary folks. Although we clearly have classes in our society we often pretend that we don't and harbor the illusion that social mobility is so great that anybody with talent can reach the top through hard work.

Let's be frank. *The People* is a largely meaningless term as Americans use it. It does not fit any particular demographic profile. The People are the poor, the middle class, and the young and the old. That is, they are everybody and therefore nobody in particular. Thus things stand today, and thus things have stood since the founding. James Madison conceded in private that there is no such thing as The People. America is not a mass, no single group can claim to be representative, and majorities shift constantly. Even though the Constitution was promulgated in the name of "We the People," the construct was a fiction of the drafters' imagination. It presupposed the existence of a single public interest that simply cannot exist in a country as large as ours in which there are numerous competing interests. One of Madison's keenest insights was that this diversity of interests, far from being a liability, is a handmaiden of liberty. Where multiple interests compete, no single interest can dominate. But in public Madison could be less than candid. During the ratification debates in Virginia, the historian Joseph Ellis tells us, Madison argued that the reference in the Constitution to "the people" denoted the people of the various states. This was an argument of sheer expediency. Patrick Henry, the leader of the Virginia anti-federalists, had charged that the drafters had deliberately set out to undermine state authority by claiming to act on behalf of The People. Madison's response was specifically shaped to put the fears of people like Henry to rest.

Madison may have been one of the first politicians to discover the usefulness of that endlessly elastic term: *The People*. He was hardly the last. Remember Al Gore's campaign slogan, "The People versus the powerful"? John Kerry liked it so much he recycled it four years later. Every politician claims to represent The People. To the politician the phrase—almost always it is not just The People, but The American People—is a classic throwaway line with a pleasant populist tinge. Likely as not, the politician who repeats it includes it out of habit, using the phrase because everybody does: both the conservative pol who wants to destroy Social Security and the liberal pol who wants to save it. In 1968 both Lyndon Johnson in speeches in favor of the Vietnam War and Eugene McCarthy in speeches opposing the war expressed their confidence in The People's wisdom:

EUGENE MCCARTHY (after his stupendous showing in the New Hampshire primary in which he challenged LBJ for the nomination): "There were many who said our system could not be made responsible to this kind of challenge, that this democracy did not have the strength among its people to stand in mid-course against a policy, which was in progress, and to say this policy is wrong and something must be done about it. Well, we did put the people to that test, and I think it's clear they have met the test."

LYNDON JOHNSON (in his speech announcing, in the aftermath of McCarthy's surprisingly strong showing in the New Hampshire primary, that he would not be a candidate in 1968): "I believe that now, no less than when the decade began, this generation of Americans is willing to 'pay any price, bear any burden, meet any hardship, support any friend, oppose any foe to assure the survival and the success of liberty.' Since those words were spoken by John F. Kennedy, the people of America have kept that compact with mankind's noblest cause. And we shall continue to keep it."

"The People of America"! Well, it sounds good, even if the phrase is meaningless.

5

Giving Control to the People

◆

There's nothing as trustworthy . . . as the ordinary mind
of the ordinary man.

—SLOGAN OF LARRY "LONESOME" RHODES
IN THE MOVIE *A FACE IN THE CROWD*

One of the curiosities of our age is that at the very same
time that evidence began accumulating in the 1950s and
1960s that the masses are grossly ill-informed and irrational, and our politics driven by myths, the political system was reconfigured in such a way as to give the masses
more direct control than ever before.

Chiefly this came about through the ever-increasing
use of polls. Until the arrival of the modern political poll,
Washington could not rely on public opinion to guide its
every decision because there was no way of knowing what
the public's opinion was, except in a general way. Until
the 1950s one could not even begin to predict with any

degree of accuracy how voters would vote except in elections where a landslide was expected. And even then the
pollsters could get matters wrong as the experts behind
the *Literary Digest* poll of 1936 infamously did when, mis-
takenly using phone directories to produce the lists of
random survey contacts (during a time in our history
when many people lacked phones), they reached the conclusion that President Alf Landon would be replacing
Franklin Roosevelt. But polling improved. And once it
became possible to determine the public's opinion scien-
tifically, nobody stopped to ask if we should. It was assumed that we should. Not a week goes by now that we
do not have another poll to tell us what the public thinks,
feels, fears, or hopes. Google the phrase *political polls* and
in under one second you can call up 1.8 million links as I
did on 11/12/07.

Today polls dictate the national agenda, informing us
of the issues that are hot or boring, who's up and who's
down, and what's what.

The old Theory of American Politics (TAP) was rather
simple. America was like a bus. The People could tell the
driver where they want to go. They could even yell from
time to time if they saw the driver taking a wrong turn.
And of course it was presumed that any one of them could
(with a little luck and the financial backing of an array of
special interests) become a driver himself. But at no time
was it stated that The People actually should direct the
driver when to brake and when to stop, when to slow

down and when to speed up. These and a thousand other similar decisions were left up to the driver, who was presumed to possess enough good sense to steer skillfully if not always perfectly.

That was TAP. Now there's TRAP. The Theory (Revised) of American Politics is that The People should tell the driver not only where to go but when to stop, start, signal, or not signal. And if the mood strikes them they may from time to time not only yell at the driver but actually grab the wheel and try to drive the darn thing themselves, all 300 million of them, or a goodly number of them anyway. If the vehicle driven under these circumstances seems to veer and lurch and on occasion suddenly run off the road, so be it.

This is a strange way to run a country, for what attracts the attention of the public is often of little consequence. One minute it may be the trial of a mob boss, the next the death of a killer whale. While we are talking about these largely inconsequential matters, we are not talking about the consequential ones. Anybody can have an opinion about killer whales or a president's sex life. But it takes knowledge and reflection to reach a considered opinion about the budget deficit or national security. Result: We largely skip these subjects, focusing as a nation on ephemera instead.

To understand how insipid this approach to governing is, consider what would happen to a CEO who reads only the reports he finds entertaining. Could he last in the job?

The answer to the question is obviously no, he could not, unless the shareholders were prepared to see the company's stock price plummet and the company's workers were prepared to join the ranks of the unemployed. In the real world, long before things got too far out of whack, our CEO would be fired and a new chief executive installed.

We cannot fire the American people. So unless we do something to elevate the level of public debate, the hard, complicated, and often boring problems will pile up ever higher and higher. And every week Washington politicians will consult the polls to try to divine what we think, feel, fear, and hope to find out how *they* should think, feel, fear, and hope—and how they should govern us.

As I began writing this chapter in the spring of 2006, gasoline prices shot up in many places past $3 a gallon. With polls showing high gas prices as the leading concern of the American people—a *Wall Street Journal/NBC Nightly News* poll indicated that 45 percent of Americans considered high gas prices the country's no. 1 concern, ahead of Iran's nuclear program (no. 2), illegal immigration (no. 3), and even the Iraq War (no. 4)—both the president and the Congress immediately began taking steps to show that *they* are concerned. (It was an election year, after all.) On Tuesday, April 25, 2006, President Bush announced that he was (a) suspending the purchase of oil for the Strategic Petroleum Reserve, (b) relaxing environmental regulations on the formulation of gasoline, and (c) overseeing an investigation of possible price-gouging. On

Thursday, April 27, Reuters reported that Senate Republicans wanted to "soften the blow of rapidly rising gasoline prices by giving taxpayers a $100 check and suspending a retail fuel tax." Doubts immediately surfaced in the press that any of these steps would have much of an impact. The *New York Times* reported that oil experts believed that the president actually had little ability to affect the price of gasoline. "Every little bit does help," oil analyst Phil Flynn told NBC News, "but it doesn't get any littler than this." According to Flynn, Bush's moves were likely to add at best some 15,000 barrels a day to the nation's oil stream, a pittance given that the United States was using 21 million barrels of oil a day. But the point was to show the public that *something* was being done, not to implement wise policies that might actually address the underlying forces driving prices up. And nobody in Washington was saying that high gasoline prices might be the thing to jump-start a much-needed conservation movement.

For years conservationists have been howling about the risk to the country of our high oil consumption. But since the public was uninterested in the problem, the politicians in Washington were uninterested. Or worse—they were afraid of confronting the problem. Any solution undoubtedly would involve higher taxes on energy to curb demand. No rational politician chose to stir up that politically lethal hornet's nest.

It is possible that politicians in Washington would have responded just as they did in April 2006 without polls.

Anecdotal evidence surely would have convinced them that the rise in gas prices was a subject of intense interest. But before polling became commonplace, Washington had more freedom to react to events according to its own timetable. With new polls coming out almost daily, today the city has to respond to public concerns immediately, with politicians committing to policies that their aides dream up in an instant, even if upon reflection other policies might be more suitable. Certainly the process is more democratic, but that it is prudent is doubtful.

The public, showing unexpected common sense, rejected the solutions proffered by the pols. Bush's non-plan plan was seen for what it was, driving his numbers further southward. According to an AP-Ipsos poll released on May 5, 2006, just 23 percent approved of the way he was "handling gas prices," a new low. The Senate Republican plan to write us $100 checks accomplished the neat trick of attracting the scorn of both liberals and conservatives. Rush Limbaugh told listeners on his radio show that the senators were "treating us like we're a bunch of whores." Five days after the plan was announced it was withdrawn.

Polling has become so much a part of American politics that presidents now put pollsters on the White House payroll and newscasts lead with the results of polls. Clothes may be the measure of the ordinary man, but to a pol what counts are his poll numbers. If they are up, he is on top of the world, able to command attention and respect. Down, and he has trouble getting his calls returned.

In early 2006, as President Bush's poll numbers dropped to 35 percent, members of his own party began distancing themselves from him. One Republican candidate even had the temerity suddenly to discover that he had a scheduling conflict when the president showed up to attend a fundraiser being held on the candidate's own behalf.

Never before have the public's opinions (confused or not) been so well known. And never before have political leaders deferred to public opinion as much as our leaders have in the last generation. Rather than being the beginning point of a national debate, a poll is often regarded as the final word, as if Moses himself had spoken. "The American people already made their decision," Vice President Dick Cheney said in March 2006, alluding to polls indicating that a majority of Americans approved of the president's decision to eavesdrop on certain calls without a warrant. "They agree with the president." Cheney's unspoken message? Once The People have made their views clear through the polls, public criticism is unwarranted. Ergo, Democrats should cease criticizing Mr. Bush forthwith. After all, on what basis could they grumble in dissent? The Democrats did back off. (It wasn't Cheney who was a slave to public opinion, it was the Democrats.)

I do not want to leave the impression that politicians rarely take a position in opposition to the polls. Studies show that they do on a regular basis when they feel they can get away with it. One study of the gap between what politicians do and what the polls say found that it grew

larger between 1981 and 1993 than it had been in the
1970s. There are a variety of reasons for this. One may
simply be that incumbency is now so taken for granted
(few members of Congress have to worry about losing re-
election) that the pressure to follow the polls may be less
acute. Or it may be that the research is incomplete. Measuring the gap is difficult.

From what politicians say, constant polling has become
a terrible burden, robbing public service of much of its
joy. A politician has to walk carefully now to avoid the risk
of alienating important groups whose disenchantment can
be measured in an instant ("plus or minus four points")
with the near-precision of a blood pressure monitor. In
such an environment the pol often feels besieged. Yet
what alternative is there? No wonder Bill Clinton ended
up taking a poll to tell him where to vacation. If one could
take a poll to find out what people think, why wouldn't
one even if it is emasculating? (And it's emasculating only
if the public finds out about the poll.)

At the same time that polling took root, so did primaries. They too added to the power of ordinary voters.
They were first employed on the national level in a limited fashion in the election of 1912 at the insistence of
Progressive reformers. But the bosses quickly struck back
and that ended that. In the '50s a new crowd of reformers again championed primaries and over time primaries
became a fixed part of American politics. In 1960 under
40 percent of the delegates to the national conventions

were selected in primaries. By 1968 almost half were. The Democratic Party debacle in Chicago in 1968 ushered in a period of feverish change. Furious that Hubert Humphrey had been able to win the party's nomination with the support of old-style bosses, reformers changed the rules to increase the number and power of ordinary delegates. By 1976, 70 percent of the delegates were chosen in primaries; by 1992, more than 85 percent were. Instead of the bosses selecting the party's nominees, now the voters would.*

Another democratic development has been the increasing use of referendums and initiatives. These, too, had their origins in the Progressive Era, but it is in our own that they have become ubiquitous. In 2006 alone, eighty-one citizen initiatives were put on the ballot in more than twenty states. Legislatures, likewise, have been putting measures directly before the voters in ever increasing numbers on all sorts of subjects, from immigration to taxes and even foreign policy. In 2007 the California legislature approved SB 924 to give voters the opportunity in the 2008 primary to say if they wanted U.S. troops to be withdrawn from Iraq immediately. (Governor Arnold Schwarzenegger—who first won his office when the previous governor was recalled by the citizens in a special

---

* The last candidate to win his party's nomination without winning a majority of the primaries was Gerald Ford in 1976. Ronald Reagan won seven primaries, Ford four.

election, yet another example of people power—vetoed the measure.)

These three developments—polling, primaries, and referendums—are a natural consequence of the democratic forces unleashed in the American Revolution by the demand for government by common consent. As John Adams wearily noted, with the enshrinement of the principle that The People are sovereign, group after group would now get in line demanding to be heard. Soon blacks would want to be consulted, then women, and who knew who else? Adams was too much a figure of the eighteenth century to welcome this prospect, though his wife Abigail was hopeful it would lead to the empowerment of women. Don't forget the ladies, she told him.

But should we be cheering on these recent democratic developments? We have put our fate in the hands of The People, the same folks who by and large (1) find politics boring and (2) are ignorant and irrational about public affairs.

How come, if we have been getting more democratic over the last few decades, it often feels as if we have been getting less democratic? This is one of the paradoxes of our time. But it is easily explained.

First, the public's opinion about issues is usually muddled. In the absence of a strong and overwhelming consensus, politicians can often chart a course that seems responsive to enough people to pass muster even if it really isn't, leaving many disgruntled. A good example of this was President Bush's escalation of the Iraq War in 2007. At the beginning of the year it was evident that the public was becoming tired of the war. Most people wanted out. But because the public did not have a fixed idea of how to get out or how quickly to do it, President Bush was able to convince enough people to give his new strategy a chance to avoid a massive public revolt—as long as he did something! By the fall of 2007 he was able to play up enough positive statistics to make people think the war was going well—or well enough to be forgotten. A *New York Times* poll of Iowa voters found in November 2007 that even among Democrats only 36 percent considered the war their number-one concern (among Republicans the figure was lower: just 13 percent). Anti-war activists stewed that the president was ignoring public opinion. But what actually happened was that he had successfully manipulated public opinion. This isn't the same thing as ignoring it.

One of the ironies of our time is that polls are themselves a form of manipulation in the hands of strategists who know how to use them to frame issues in a way that meets with the public's approbation. Polls are used by politicians not only to figure out what the public wants but how to sell them a policy the politician has already settled on. As political scientist Alan Wolfe says, "In the old politics of democracy, opinion was the input and policy the outcome. In the new politics of democracy, it is the reverse."

Another reason millions feel that the country is becoming less democratic is that in a very real way it is. Special interests today often have an iron grip on the federal government. Lobbying the government has become a small industry. Between 2000 and 2005 the number of registered lobbyists in Washington D.C. doubled to nearly 35,000.

How, then, can we square what is happening in Washington with the claim that the people are more powerful than ever before? In all those subjects in which the public takes a direct and lively interest, it has become superpowerful. But the number of subjects about which the public has a clear opinion is tiny. This gives special interests an edge they exploit to the maximum. Because people do not follow what is happening in Congress closely, lobbyists are able to win breaks for their clients and manipulate the system to their advantage. By virtue of the wealth at the disposal of special interests, they are in a position as well to make enormous campaign contributions and to hire high-priced lobbyists, many of whom formerly served with the people they are now seeking to influence. In addition, and this is the truly insidious part, special interests can finance advertising campaigns to shape public opinion on issues they care about (like the "Harry and Louise" commercials the insurance industry financed in 1993 to sabotage support for the Clinton healthcare plan). These advertisements can have a dramatic impact on how the voters think because the latter are so uninformed.

This chapter tells an ugly, disconcerting story. What about the Internet? Could this fascinating tool give us the happy ending we are so desperate for? While there is some reason to hope that the Internet may over time have a positive effect on our democracy, the record thus far is less than encouraging. While in theory the Internet gives ordinary voters the opportunity to participate in politics, in practice it has been used mainly by true believers to advance their particular agendas. The effect has been to make our politics more polarized than ever, as politicians cater to those on the margins rather than in the center. In Madisonian theory, as more people become involved in politics, true believers will have less and less of a chance to dominate. But so far not enough people have joined the groups that use the Internet to provide the balance that's needed.

6

The Power of Television

◆

Don't shoot too high, aim lower, and the common
people will understand you.
—ATTRIBUTED TO ABRAHAM LINCOLN

At the same time that people were being given more control, television suddenly and dramatically became a relentless force in politics. The timing was a disaster. For
television makes people dumber. In short, people got
more power than ever before at the precise moment that
television made them less likely than in the past to be able
to exercise power responsibly.

There is one thing you can say about the marriage of
television and politics: They seemed made for each
other. Unfortunately, they got serious before either understood the consequences, which were unsavory for
both of them.

Oh, but how sweet it all was in those first few years of early courting. Colonel Theodore Roosevelt, Jr., governor-general of the Philippines and son of the late president, writing in 1932, predicted that TV will "stir the nation to a lively interest in those who are directing its policies and in the policies themselves" by bringing politics into the home. "The result will normally be that we may expect more intelligent, more concerted action from an electorate; the people will think more for themselves and less simply at the direction of local members of the political machines."

Orrin Dunlap, Jr., the first television correspondent of the *New York Times*, claimed in 1940 that, with television, "trickery has less chance to operate" because cameras now would be focusing on the "lights and shadows of politics." Television would lead to the elimination of "hokus pokus" in politics. "Sincerity of the tongue and facial expression gain in importance. More than ever, as the politician chieftains observe, 'we are approaching the dawn of clear, intelligent politics.'" Better yet: Candidates would be "nominated in front of the people; not in a smoke-filled hotel room where politicians of the past are said to have bartered and hatched history."

Thomas Dewey, the presidential candidate of the Republican Party in 1944 and 1948, said that "television is an X-ray. If a man doesn't know the business of government, he cannot long stand its piercing lights and stark realism. It should make a constructive advance in political campaigning."

With little concern for the possible pitfalls that might surface once they got to know each other a little better, both parties—politics and TV—plunged forward, exchanged their vows, and said "I do." This proved unfortunate in the long run for both of them. But for a time they got along splendidly. The pols provided drama and excitement, and television provided an audience. As long as the pol had a touch of the actor he did well and both were happy.

FDR, the first president to appear on the tube, was a model TV president. He had perfect timing. He smiled a lot. And he knew how to strike a pose without seeming to strike a pose. That is, he knew how to act naturally, which takes real talent. One news reporter put it this way after FDR's television debut in 1936:

> As [the president] nodded and smiled through space there could be no doubt that he will excel as a television "actor," for his magnetic smile and magnificent radio voice make an ideal combination for telecasting. It would seem that the art of smiling is now likely to be cultivated as much as the voice is for broadcasting. But just as there are natural-born voices for radio, so no doubt there will be captivating smiles, and they will count more than the forced smile, which by television seems to speed through space as an affected grin. Naturalness is to be a keynote of success before the "seeing-microphone," as the radio-camera is called. President Roosevelt's telecasts are proof of this.

As television execs immediately grasped, politics provided a never-ending stream of dramatic events ideal for the cameras and the little box: political conventions, candidate debates, election nights, and presidential inaugurations. The only apparent downside at first was that not all politicians were up to television's dramatic demands. In 1940 when the Republican Party's national convention was broadcast—a first—the audience had to endure a droning speech by Herbert Hoover. Toward the end of his speech, the cameramen pleaded with Hoover to smile. He refused. His newspaper reviews the next day were commensurate with his performance:

> [The Convention chairman] rushed up to try to save the day; he lifted high the arm of Mr. Hoover. . . . It could not be said that the ex-President was bored, but he did not seem to know exactly how to play the role. The band pounded away; his cohorts yelled. The effort to start a stampede on the floor petered out after a few banners were seen to move in the aisles. Mr. Hoover as a telecaster gained no more than he ever did as a broadcaster.

The reviews were a sign that pols in the modern age would have to be cut from a different mold than Mr. Hoover. Fortunately, the supply of solid television performers was seemingly endless. Not once since the dawn of the television age has there been a serious concern that we might run out.

But by and by, little signs emerged that trouble lay ahead as TV and the bosses struggled for control. The first tussle came in 1948 when TV execs began to assert the power to select the city in which the political conventions would be held, a power reserved to party bosses for more than a century. As the execs explained, the only coaxial cable in the country at the time extended from New York City to Philadelphia. If the bosses wanted their conventions covered live, they had to put them in Philly. The execs complained bitterly that four years earlier, when both conventions had been held in Chicago, footage of the day's events had to be shipped to New York by airplane each afternoon at 2 P.M. to be ready for broadcast that evening. This had cost a small fortune and robbed the proceedings of the feeling of immediacy. To make a real impression on the nation's viewers—by 1948 some 10 million watched some of the political conventions on television—the proceedings would have to be covered live.

The bosses caved.

The next blow to the old order came in 1951 with the Kefauver crime hearings. Estes Kefauver was a little-known junior senator from Tennessee who had been elected just three years earlier. But as the head of the Senate Special Committee to Investigate Crime in Interstate Commerce, he became a media sensation. His hearings, drawing millions of viewers, were broadcast live in many of the cities where they were held. Jack Gould, the television critic of the *Times*, noted that in New York "housewives have left the housework undone and husbands have slipped away from their jobs to watch. The city has been under a hypnotic spell, absorbed, fascinated, angered and amused. It has been a rare community experience."

By the time the hearings ended, a small number of people had become national celebrities. There was the mobster Frank Costello, whose twisting hands had been featured in close-ups after he refused to allow the cameras to focus on his face while he testified. And there was the Senate committee's chief attorney, who used his newfound fame to win a seat as president of the New York City Council. But most important there was Kefauver. Kefauver was now so big a national figure that he felt he could challenge the power of the bosses (with whom he'd never gotten along—as the mayor of Memphis he had tangled with Boss E. H. Crump) and run for president of the United States in 1952. This didn't go over well with the bosses, who in the past had always decided who ran for president. Who did Kefauver think he was to decide on a run on his own? Yet that spring Kefauver proved a powerhouse. Entering eleven primaries, he won ten of them, defeating Truman in the New Hampshire contest. By the arrival of the Democratic National Convention, Kefauver had more popular support than any other Democrat.

In any previous era it would have been impossible for a candidate lacking the support of the bosses to contemplate a run. But television changed the arithmetic of American politics. An ambitious pol who had gotten his face on television could be taken seriously as a candidate simply because voters by the millions had learned his name and liked him. Say what you will about the bosses, they had never picked a candidate for president based solely on name familiarity and personal appeal. They had always considered the résumés of potential candidates, too, as they did in 1944 when they insisted on putting Harry Truman in as Roosevelt's running mate. Aware that FDR was dying, they connived to give the second spot to a person they had confidence could take over if necessary—and they had great confidence in Truman, who had won universal respect as chairman of the Senate committee investigating corruption and malfeasance during World War II. (The bosses had no confidence in the incumbent vice president, Henry Wallace, who dabbled in mysticism.) But Kefauver was a pol with no résumé to speak of who suddenly was considered a contender.

And they weren't the only pols to find TV objectionable. So did Truman, who considered Kefauver a lightweight. In a White House press release Truman made his views as clear as the picture of a GE Model 802D, one of the era's popular television sets:

[T]he President thinks highly of television. He insists on full use of it in all of his major speeches. The President has real misgivings, however, about the use of television at hearings because of the tendency to make Roman holidays of them. One day he observed that one of the major factors in the weakening of the governments of Athens and of other democratic Greek states was the adoption of trial by mass jury. In that way emotions sway over reason. Socrates was tried in that way and the result was most unfair. On this the President is most seriously concerned. The trouble with television hearings, he said, is that a man is held before cameras and 40,000,000 people more or less hear him charged with so and so, and the public, untrained generally with evaluating the presentation of evidence, is inclined to think him guilty just because he is charged. Then the pressure begins mounting on the committee and the result can be that the witness is pushed around. It is the very negation of judicial process, with the committee acting as prosecutor and defense, and the public acting as the jury.

House Speaker Sam Rayburn was asked if he wanted cameras in the Congress: "Televise sessions of the House? Hell no! Not while I'm around here."

"Can I quote you on that Mr. Speaker?" a reporter asked.

"Hell, yes."

Taking notice of the rumbling complaints reporters were starting to hear about television, the editors in the *Times* ran a story carrying the provocative headline "Political Leaders Acclaim TV But Warn Against Its Misuse."

The bosses succeeded in beating back Kefauver's challenge, but it was hard and the fight damaged the party going into the fall elections. Millions who'd become enchanted with Kefauver had had their hopes dashed when Illinois Governor Adlai Stevenson won the party's nomination.

The Republican Party bosses also became disillusioned with TV. Going into *their* convention in '52, they hoped to swing the nomination to party warhorse Robert Taft, Mr. Republican, who had been waiting patiently for years for the chance to stand in the winner's circle. Conservatives especially were hopeful. For twenty years they had been forced to sit back while the party nominated one moderate after another in hopes of weaning away middle-of-the-road Democrats from the New Deal coalition. Finally, the party seemed to have its best shot in a generation for victory. Truman was down to 23 percent in the polls. The war in Korea was going badly. And people seemed hungry for change. Once again moderate forces in the party were rallying around another moderate, Dwight Eisenhower, who appeared to be in much the same mold as Alf Landon, Wendell Willkie, and Thomas Dewey, the nominees since Hoover. But Taft seemed as likely as Ike to win in November if only he could get the nomination. Then in the opening days of the convention Eisenhower won a decisive TV battle orchestrated by the savvy Herbert Brownell, Dewey's campaign manager, that would give Ike the nomination instead of Taft. At a critical meeting of the national committee, which was faced with two slates from Texas, one pro-Taft, one pro-Eisenhower, Taft's forces objected to the presence of television cameras. Brownell, seizing the opportunity, argued that Taft was attempting to sidestep the democratic process to cheat Ike out of the nomination. Once people had become accustomed to television they expected to be able to watch events unfold on television. And here was Mr. Republican trying to block their access. This gave Ike's team a decisive PR advantage. And of course Ike went on to win both the nomination and the election.

Thus far in our brief history it has seemed that however rocky the marriage of TV and politics may have been, it was good for The People. At least, it seemed good for The People if you believe that boss power is bad and that any diminution of boss power is a positive. In each conflict surveyed above, the bosses lost power and The People gained power whenever the outcome of events was determined by television. But the net result was that power shifted from the folks who knew the most about politics to people who often knew little.

It is the fall of '52. The campaigns are in full swing. Out of the blue, in mid-September, the *New York Post* features a screaming headline about the Republican vice presidential candidate: "Secret Rich Men's Trust Fund Keeps Nixon in Style Far Beyond His Salary." According to the *Post*, Richard Nixon has been keeping a slush fund provided by rich friends to help him meet personal expenses. As slush funds go, this one was actually pretty small, at least by our standards: $18,000 and change. And in fact it wasn't a slush fund at all. Nixon used the money to pay for legitimate expenses related to his political duties. He did not use the money to buy gifts for his wife Pat or to pay his personal bills, but the public reaction was robust enough that some thought Nixon might have to be replaced. Eisenhower, who had designed his campaign around the theme that the Democrats were corrupt, was sufficiently alarmed by the ruckus that he declined to issue a statement of support. Nixon himself was convinced he would be cast aside unless he could rally public opinion quickly. He settled on a prime-time television speech that became famous for the name of the Nixon family dog, Checkers. Nixon talked about his wife's good Republican cloth coat. He talked about his kids. And of course he brought up their dog:

> One other thing I probably should tell you, because if I don't they'll probably be saying this about me, too—we did get something, a gift, after the election. . . . [T]he day before we left on this campaign trip, we got a message from the Union Station in Baltimore, saying they had a package for us. It was a little cocker-spaniel dog . . . and our little girl Tricia, the six-year-old, named it Checkers. And you know the kids, like all kids, love the dog and . . . regardless of what they say about it, we're going to keep it.

Thirty million people tuned in to watch the speech— the largest television audience any show had yet attracted.

Liking what they saw, they rallied to Nixon's side. Ike then issued the most famous, if also most condescending, endorsement in American political history: "Dick, you're my boy."

The net effect of this television mini-drama? Power once again shifted from the party to The People. It was not the bosses who decided Nixon should stay or go. It was not even Ike. It was the masses.

The day after the speech Jack Gould, from his perch at the *Times*, berated Nixon for the way in which he had used television. "There is enough emotionalism in a campaign under the best of circumstances," Gould wrote, "without using it as a premeditated policy and tactic. If either Republicans or Democrats should tread on the edge of demagoguery, in the long run it will be the country that will suffer and television's usefulness will be dangerously impaired."

Continuing on, it is October now. The country is debating the issues of the day: Korea, corruption, and all the rest. Where is Dwight David Eisenhower? We find him in a television studio reciting lines off a cue card scripted by Madison Avenue advertiser Rosser Reeves, the man who invented the M&Ms slogan "Melts in your mouth, not in your hand." We are present at the birth of the political version of the thirty-second commercial: the spot. In one spot, a voter asks Ike, "Are we going to have to fight another war?" The general answers: "No, not if we have a sound program for peace. And I'll add this, we won't spend hundreds of billions and still not have enough tanks and planes for Korea."

It is as superficial as politics gets. And Ike knows it. As he walks off the studio set, he is heard muttering, "To think that an old soldier should come to this!" But superficiality is what television politics is all about. It is about the candidate's smile and sincerity. It is about slogans. It is about clever packaging. As Rosser Reeves explained to fellow Republicans, the average viewer cannot take in more than one idea at a time. After listening to a speech by even a great orator like Winston Churchill, what does the casual listener remember? He remembers at best a few words such as Churchill's warning that an iron curtain was descending across Eastern Europe. Therefore, in Reeves's view, there was nothing wrong with the thirty-second spot. It merely reflected the reality that viewers can absorb only so much.

Adlai Stevenson resisted running spots. After seeing the Eisenhower ads, he exploded: "I don't think the American people want politics and the presidency to become the plaything of the high-pressure men, of the ghostwriters, of the public relations men. I think they will be shocked by such contempt for the intelligence of the American people. This isn't soap opera, this isn't Ivory Soap versus Palmolive." But four years later, in his rematch with the general, Stevenson too ran spots.

Once again the parties grew weaker, but this time power shifted from the bosses to Stevenson's "high-pressure men" instead of to The People. Say you were a candidate running for office. Knowing that television could make the difference in whether you were elected or sent home packing, whom would you think to sign up first: Joe Blow Party Boss or the slick Madison Avenue magician who knew how to design a powerful spot that could attract broad support? Once television became an established institution, the magicians assumed in part the role formerly held by the bosses. Now it was *they* who could, by choosing to back one candidate over another, virtually decide which candidate would be put before the voters. With the right magician's stamp of approval, a candidate could raise funds, attract media attention, and begin measuring the drapes of his or her new office. Unlike the old party bosses, however, the magicians had no direct links to the voters. Say what you will about the bosses, they always did. Their power depended on servicing voters' needs directly: getting a street paved, the garbage picked up, or a relative a new job.

Since candidates now often selected themselves, as Kefauver had, the party was mainly left with the responsibility of raising the sums needed to buy television time and to pay for the making of television commercials, sums that were always vast. Those Eisenhower spots? They cost $2 million in 1952 when a million dollars was still a lot of money. The more the parties focused on raising money, the less time they had for anything else. Today party leaders race around the country like Mafia bagmen picking up cash from the rich folks who are willing to bankroll television campaigns.

Television alone didn't kill the old party system. There were multiple factors in its demise. The birth of modern suburbia weakened the old inner-city machines. Civil service reforms limited the number of jobs that bosses could hand out. And the more educated people became, the less susceptible they were to mindless appeals to "party loyalty." But if you had to pick one cause, television was probably as good as any.

Many of the newspaper ads for the first television sets to roll off the assembly lines used as a selling point the fact that television gave the average person the chance to see politics up close. Buy a Stromberg-Carlson, proclaimed one ad, and you "can see and hear more of the Presidential Conventions than the delegates themselves. . . . You're in the scenes and behind the scenes—with history in the making!" An ad for GE's Model 802D proclaimed, "See History Made When They Pick Their Man for the World's Biggest Job." WJZ TV, the ABC affiliate in New York, boasted: "These are thrilling historic days; and, thanks to the magic of television, the great events of '48 will happen in front of your eyes."

The impossible-to-ignore moral of these ads was that the viewer no longer needed the party bosses or anyone else to give him the inside dope on the conventions. He could watch them himself and draw his own conclusions. Because television gave the viewers a "front-row seat" in politics, voters by the millions became persuaded that they no longer needed the parties for political guidance and proudly proclaimed their independence. Between 1952 and 1988 party loyalty declined from 75 percent to 63 percent.

Ordinary voters do not seem to have been frightened by their isolation. They should have been.

In a careful study Kurt and Gladys Lang arranged for three groups of viewers to watch the 1952 Democratic Convention. One group watched NBC, another ABC, and another CBS. Through content analysis the Langs determined that all three networks presented, with minor exceptions, the same basic information. But each network approached the conventions differently. NBC focused on personalities, leaving analysis largely up to the newspapers. (The network's motto: "Let the pictures speak for themselves.") ABC emphasized non-stop action and inside scoops. CBS, taking the risk that it would bore viewers, stuck to a dry approach, telling viewers what was happening as it happened with analysis as needed. As one senior CBS producer told the Langs, "It's not up to us to make it a good show."

To the Langs' surprise, the way the networks covered the convention decisively shaped the impressions of viewers. NBC viewers seized on the seemingly rude manner in which Sam Rayburn presided. When he refused to recognize a delegate who wanted to make a motion to adjourn, they drew the conclusion that he was being impolite, failing to understand that he was actually trying to give the politicians time to work out a deal. ABC viewers came away confused because the network's jumpy coverage (a result of its constant search for riveting footage and scoops) made it difficult to follow the action. But they, too, focused on Rayburn, concluding that he had ruled in an arbitrary manner. Only CBS viewers, informed step by step why Rayburn acted as he did, had a rational understanding of the proceedings. Properly, "they interpreted what they saw . . . as a showdown among several factions with Rayburn trying to mediate."

What the Langs' study demonstrated was that television didn't necessarily give viewers a better grasp of the intricacies of politics as critics had hoped. TV was indeed just as likely to give them a warped and misleading view as a sound one. And as the networks became increasingly concerned with ratings and the producers consequently began to emphasize personalities and action (precisely the approaches taken by NBC and ABC in 1952 that had left viewers so confused), there was every reason to think that viewers would become less well informed rather than more.

Social scientists, oddly enough, were at first confounded by this development. While politicians like FDR worried about the impact of the mass media on voters and took elaborate measures to regulate radio and television, researchers believed that there was abundant evidence that voters were hard-wired to resist manipulation, possessing as it were a kind of DNA gene for stubbornness. Human beings, instead of being persuaded by the mass media, tend to heed only those messages that conform with their pre-existing views, it was believed. That is, they filter out messages that conflict with their established opinions. As evidence the social scientists pointed to the election of 1928. That year the Democratic candidate, Al Smith, ran an aggressive radio advertising campaign, the first in history. Millions listened intently to Smith's appeals on their new-fangled radios. Then in November they voted in droves—for Herbert Hoover.

Social scientists expected television viewers to react just as radio listeners had. As one researcher put it in 1957, "before [a voter] even sits down to the television set, he is prepared to react in a preset way to whatever comes out of it." That is, "[m]an is far from a *tabula rasa*, or clean slate, for mass communication to write on. . . . He has built up a sense of values which lead him to react positively or negatively to much of what the candidate will say." Then came the first great test of television's ability to change people's minds. And it turned out that television seemed actually to shape and reshape viewers' perceptions.

The test took place on the night of September 26, 1960, at 9 P.M. (EST) in the studios of WBBM in Chicago, when Richard Nixon and John Kennedy squared off before an audience of 60–70 million people in the first televised presidential debate in history. Each man gave as good as he got. Each made a coherent case for his own candidacy.

Judging from transcripts of the debates, one would be hard-pressed to say which candidate was the winner. (Of course, a debate has to have a winner. That's the point, isn't it? Which may be part of the problem. The exercise is primarily intended not to educate viewers but to persuade them. Any education they get is incidental. But I digress.)

But on television? It was a Kennedy landslide. According to the Gallup poll, Kennedy won the debate by a two-to-one margin.

What accounted for the difference between the transcripts and the actual television production? It became the stuff of television legend. Nixon looked tired. Kennedy looked rested. Nixon wore a white shirt. Kennedy wore a blue shirt, which showed up better on the black-and-white cameras of the day. Nixon looked pale and pasty. Kennedy looked tanned. Nixon sweated. Kennedy was perspiration-free. Nixon looked unsteady on his feet. Kennedy stood ramrod straight.

Is this when innocence died? Is this when the trivial in politics came to triumph over substance? The short answer is no. To say that would be going too far. Shallowness was an established part of American politics long before TV came along. But TV did more than plagiarize the worst of past campaigns. It raised manipulation to a high art. What the presidential debates of 1960—there were four in all—proved was that it is vital to work every angle you can to gain an advantage. It wasn't by accident that Nixon's pores oozed beads of sweat during one debate.

Knowing that Nixon was prone to sweating, J. Leonard Reinsch, Kennedy's media consigliere, later confessed that he contrived to raise the studio temperature in the hours before the event to make sure that when the hot lights came up the candidates would find themselves baking as if they had wandered onto the floor of the Death Valley desert: "I finally located a janitor in the second basement below the studio," Reinsch recalled. After making a series of threats, the janitor pulled the key to the thermostat from the bottom drawer of a desk: "We turned the temperature up as high as we could."

Nor was it accidental that Nixon appeared unsteady on his feet at the first debate. Recently, he had injured his knee getting into a car. The mishap required a hospital stay after his knee became infected. The Kennedy people, knowing this, wanted the candidates to stand during much of the course of the hour-long debate. Nixon, to relieve the pressure on his bad knee, had to keep shifting his weight from one side to the other.

And the famous reaction shot of Nixon mopping his brow? That was no accident. Reinsch in his memoirs wrote that he pressured the director, Frank Slingland, to take reaction shots.

> "Frank," I said, "we either get reaction shots or I'm going into the reporters' studio and tell them the Democrats have been framed."

"You don't dare!" Slingland retorted, while busily calling the camera shots.

"Try me!" I shot back.

A few minutes later, reaction shots flashed on the TV screens.

Just how significant a factor was television in the election? Based on the outcome of the first debate, one would have thought that a landslide was in the making. But in November Kennedy won in a squeaker, suggesting that voters based their votes on more than the performance of the candidates at that September presidential debate. And indeed a University of Michigan study found that the usual factors were ever present: party loyalty, the opinions of friends and family, and information about the candidates' positions. But a Roper poll found that more than half of the voters who voted said they were influenced by the debates. Another 6 percent indicated that they based their decision wholly on the debates. Of the voters in this group 72 percent voted for Kennedy. Furthermore, the Langs in a separate study found that Democrats who had voted for Eisenhower in 1952 and 1956 came home to the Democratic Party in 1960 after the first debate, suggesting that television actually did affect how people voted. Kennedy himself always believed that television was critical. "We wouldn't have had a prayer," he said, "without that gadget."

Some gadget. Within a few years voters were gaining most of what they know about the candidates from television. By 1963 Americans were relying on television instead of newspapers as the primary source of news. Suddenly how a person looked and talked counted for more than what they had accomplished. In his memoir, *Six Crises*, Nixon recounted that after the first debate with Kennedy he asked his secretary, Rose Mary Woods, how he had done. She said her parents had called from Ohio to ask if Nixon was ill. On TV he looked sick. "I asked Rose what she thought. She said she tended to agree with their reaction, despite the fact that she thought I had the better of the argument on substance." Concluded Nixon: "I had concentrated too much on substance and not enough on appearance. I should have remembered that 'a picture is worth a thousand words.'" Self-serving as this comment was, it happened to be correct.

The pols adapted. In 1960 Nixon had scorned his TV handlers, refusing even to work with them on the day of that first debate. In 1968 Nixon put the TV and ad folks in charge of his campaign, hiring many of his leading staff people from the agency where aide H. R. Haldeman worked. No one again was going to outdo Richard M. Nixon in superficiality.

Nixon, thanks to Joe McGinniss's *The Selling of the President*, the best-seller that provided an inside look at "Tricky Dick's" slick advertising campaign in 1968, is remembered as the president who first used television to manipulate viewers. In the book McGinniss produced a memo by Nixon speech writer Ray Price that told the cold hard truth about the new medium: "It's not what's there that counts, it's what's projected—and carrying it one step further, it's not what *he* [Nixon] projects but rather what the voter receives."

But it was actually the much-revered JFK who understood ahead of everybody else how to use TV to win over the voters. As a senator he got himself on *Meet the Press* to embellish his credentials as a Serious Person. He got himself and Jackie on Edward R. Murrow's personality show, *Person to Person*, to show that he was a regular family man like Mr. and Mrs. Average American. He went on the *Jack Paar Show* to demonstrate his wit and charm.

In an article in *TV Guide* in 1959, Kennedy professed that television could not be used to manipulate voters even as he used it for just that purpose. "Honesty, vigor, compassion, intelligence—the presence or lack of these and other qualities make up what is called the candidate's image,'" he wrote. "My own conviction," he added, "is that these images or impressions are likely to be uncannily correct." This was blather and Kennedy knew it. In the very years that he was making claims like this he was projecting an image of himself as a family man while he cheated regularly on his wife.

TV was worse than manipulative. It was shallow. If the one thing voters remember from that first debate was that Nixon looked pale, what did they take away from later debates? From the Ford-Carter debates in 1976 it was Ford's error in saying that under a Ford administration Eastern Europe would never fall under communist influence. From the Reagan-Carter debate in 1980 it was Reagan's line "There you go again." From the Bush-Ferraro debate in 1984 it was Bush's off-the-cuff comment immediately afterward that he had kicked a little ass. From the Clinton-Bush-Perot debates in 1992 it was the moment when Bush was caught glancing at his watch as if he were bored. From the Bush-Gore debates in 2000 it was Gore's huffing and puffing. From the Bush-Kerry debates in 2004 it was the suspicious-looking bulge in the back of Bush's suit that prompted bloggers to wonder if he were taking secret directions from Karl Rove as he gave his answers.

After the debates the networks ask viewers who won and why. "I liked his smile," someone would say about candidate X. Or "Gee, Y sure looked strong." And so on and so on.

The pundits reassuringly told the *New York Times* after the third Bush-Kerry debate in October 2004 that the debate was helpful in addressing matters of substance. Presidential historian Michael Beschloss was quoted as saying, "You could have watched these debates and not known much about them and known a lot by the end—what their views are on the size of government, how they want to use force, and also how they would relate to the American people if they had to go on television and ask the American people for sacrifice." But when *Times* reporters asked college students their impressions, the comments were dismally cursory. "It comforts me to hear the president say he prays," said one. "George Bush had to look human, and he did," said another. A third student, taking note of an issue of substance, observed that Bush had indicated he is pro-life, but then added that the president "came across as more human instead of just another politician," as if what really mattered was his performance. It was indeed Bush's performance that really did matter.

Even the newspapers conceded that what mattered were the theatrical elements. Before the first Bush-Gore debate, the *Times* ran an op-ed by Kennedy speechwriter Richard N. Goodwin offering the candidates tips. A pull-quote summed up the advice: "Practice the words, but master the music." After the debate the *Times*'s headline read "Gore's Image: Focused and Relentless." After the first Bush-Kerry debate in 2004 the paper published the headline "Day After Debate, Campaigns Assess the Performances." After the third debate the *Times* went with the headline "A Television Event That Delivered High Drama and Garnered High Ratings."

One wonders how the Lincoln-Douglas debates would have been headlined had they been televised. Would the newspapers have skipped the arguments over slavery to focus on Lincoln's unkempt hairdo and Douglas's paunch? One's mind reels at the possibility that national policy about slavery might have been determined by the viewers' reaction to Lincoln's high-pitched voice or Douglas's short stature. It may be that television would have destroyed both men's careers. Standing on the same platform, the six-foot-three Lincoln next to the five-foot-four Douglas, undoubtedly would have made each look ridiculous. And people surely would have commented on it. True, viewers also would have commented on the men's personalities. But how reassuring is that?

Pundits have tried to make a virtue of the voters' focus on personality by claiming that personality is what really counts, particularly in a president. But this is a delusion. Personality is just one of several vital factors that need to be taken into account by a rational voter. Other factors include character (not the same as personality), experience, judgment, and ideology. Neither Jimmy Carter's enticing smile nor George W. Bush's down-home style, which seemed attractive on television, gave the voter solid clues as to their performance as president. In this way television misleads people. It gives them confidence that, because they can see the candidates, they "know" who they really are. This is nonsense.

Combining the worst characteristics of television is the spot, which both Eisenhower and Stevenson held in contempt. In the '50s, though some spots took a negative approach, vilifying opponents—one in 1956 by the Stevenson campaign, playing on fears about Eisenhower's health, asked, "Nervous about Nixon? President Nixon?"—it was not until 1964 that Madison Avenue consultants contemplated Extreme Advertising, conjuring up the famous Daisy Spot, in which a little girl counts off the petals of a daisy as the announcer hints that Barry Goldwater is likely to plunge the country into a nuclear war. *Three, two, one . . . Kaboom!* The Daisy Spot actually ran just once because LBJ promptly yanked it. But it set a precedent, which political consultants were eager to embrace. In 1968 the Nixon campaign put out an ad in which pictures of a smiling Hubert Humphrey were woven into wordless clips from the Vietnam War, poverty-stricken Appalachia, and the Chicago Democratic Convention street riots. Smile. War. Smile. Poverty. Smile. Riots. By 1988, reports Kathleen Hall Jamieson in her magisterial history of political commercials *Packaging the Presidency*, the ads for the first time were featuring out-and-out lies. Thus did we go from Ike and his cue cards to Bush I and Willy Horton.

In 1988 George H.W. Bush going into the election was, at one juncture, sixteen points behind his opponent, Massachusetts Governor Michael Dukakis. How to make up the difference? Bush did it by running one of the nastiest political campaigns in American history. In the "Revolving Door" ad, which focused on the Massachusetts furlough program backed by Dukakis, the Bush campaign falsely implied, reports Jamieson, that "Dukakis had furloughed 268 first degree murderers who had gone on to commit other crimes." Actually, over the period of a decade just four had escaped while on furlough, and only one had committed a major crime, the infamous Willy

Horton, who kidnapped and raped someone. A Harris poll in October indicated that 60 percent of voters had seen the Revolving Door ad. "From the time that the ad started to the time of the survey," Jamieson notes, "the percentage reporting that Dukakis was 'soft on crime' rose from 52 to 63%."

Against the great force of television what chance does the viewer have to reach a calm, dispassionate, rational view of things? Faced with a bewildering array of political spots, the viewer can consult newspapers and magazines to find out where the pols really stand on the issues. He can search the Internet for the ad watch sites that explain how the campaigns are manipulating public opinion by passing off half-truths and lies. He can check other sites to find out the names of the special interests that are paying for all those ads. And in his spare time he can keep a log of the spots that run on his favorite channels so he can go back later to remind himself of what was said and what proved to be false. But, of course, the ordinary viewer does none of these things. Instead, he watches the spots, thinks about them for a brief moment or two, then quietly absorbs whatever warped information they happen to convey. Then, if he's one of the conscientious citizens of the Republic, he casts his ballot.

Study after study shows that the spots are one of the voters' chief sources of information—and often the only source. In 2004 the University of Pennsylvania's National Annenberg Election Survey found that attack ads, the most reviled of all, convinced 61 percent of voters to believe that President George W. Bush favored "sending American jobs overseas" and 56 percent to think that Senator Kerry "voted for higher taxes 350 times." Neither claim was accurate. All Mr. Bush had said was that it "makes sense" for Americans to buy goods as cheaply as they can even if that means buying imports. Mr. Kerry's 350 votes on taxes included many that simply sustained taxes already on the books.

Americans know that the spots are manipulative. Still, even armed as we are to the hilt with suspicions, we remain unprepared to do battle with television. While familiarity with television has helped make us cynical, reinforcing the harsh lessons about the powerful learned from Vietnam, Watergate, and Iran-contra, most of us lack the sophisticated understanding of the medium needed to fully absorb the extent to which we are subject to manipulation. Lesley Stahl, the veteran CBS reporter, recalled in her autobiography that even she did not realize for many years how politicians used television to arrange and rearrange the viewers' perceptions. In 1984, when she was covering the Reagan White House, she became convinced that the administration spin machine was leaving voters with a false impression of Reagan's policies through the manipulation of visual symbols. So she produced a remarkable piece in which she laid out the facts, one after another, to blow the lid off the scam at last. "Mr. Reagan," she reported in a long piece that ran on the evening news, "tries to counter the memory of an unpopular issue with a carefully chosen backdrop that actually contradicts the president's policy. Look at the handicapped Olympics, or the opening ceremony of an old-age home. No hint that he tried to cut the budgets for the disabled and for federally subsidized housing for the elderly."

After the story ran she braced herself for criticism from the White House. Instead, she received a phone call from a Reagan official complimenting her for a "great piece." "We loved it," he said. "You what?" she responded. "We loved it!" But "how can you say you loved it—it was tough! Don't you think it was tough?" she asked. "We're in the middle of a campaign," the official explained, "and you gave us four and a half minutes of great pictures of Ronald Reagan. And that's all the American people see. . . . They don't listen to you if you're contradicting great pictures. They don't hear what you are saying if the pictures are saying something different."

Stahl finally figured it out. But how many viewers have? And what hope is there for our democracy if facts do not matter? If the image is everything, the answer would seem to be that there's not much hope at all. In a television world the pol who paints with broad brush strokes will always have it over the fellow armed with facts and figures.

The advantage of television is that the viewer can feel and experience politics. But as a transmission belt of information it is far inferior to newspapers. As TV anchorman Walter Cronkite often admitted, the network evening newscasts are a headline service. A typical show includes less information than appears on the front page of a good newspaper. It's no wonder Americans growing up in the age of television score lower on many tests measuring their political knowledge than people who grew up reading newspapers. The way television has evolved it's all but impossible for even a careful viewer of the evening newscasts, which continue to draw the largest news audiences, to gain an understanding of politics. When the shows focus on politics, something they do less and less frequently, it's the horserace they feature, not issues. Soft news trumps hard news. And sound bites run an average 9.8 seconds (compared to 42.3 seconds a generation ago). Only if viewers turn to C-SPAN do they have the opportunity to watch a politician deliver a speech in its entirety, but few bother. On cable more in-depth news stories are available, but most of the time a desire for ratings drives producers to provide entertainment rather than hard news. The talk shows on cable usually feature rants.

As for local TV news—well, if network news is superficial, local TV news is all but brain-dead.

I have been saying for years that local TV news shows make us dumber. I say this only partly for effect. They actually do appear to make us dumber because after watching a local TV news show viewers leave thinking that they actually know what's happened in their local community that day. Unfortunately, I know of no TV market in the country where this is the case.

For one thing, local TV news stations generally ignore politics, which by anybody's standards would seem to be a serious oversight. They used to cover politics. But they long ago stopped. In Seattle in 2001 during its regular Monday-through-Friday broadcasts one network TV station ran only a single packaged story (that is, a story from the field filed by a reporter) about the campaign for mayor until the day of the election. And Seattle is the most important city west of Chicago and north of San Francisco.

Having once helped run a local news department (KIRO TV, the CBS affiliate in Seattle, where I served as managing editor) I can sympathize with the news directors who refuse to broadcast stories about politics. Research proves conclusively that viewers find politics boring. And most local political stories *are* dull. Only a tiny percentage of viewers are likely to get worked up about the usual conflicts between, say, a mayor and the city council. It is hard to find a human-interest angle in stories about local politics; in fact, it is usually impossible given the time constraints under which local reporters operate. And yet human interest stories are essential because of the way the audiences for local TV newscasts are structured. The truth is they are not very local.

There are some 13,500 TV stations in the United States, which would seem to give them the opportunity to feature a lot of local stories. But the country as a whole is divided only into some 200 broadcast markets. Stations broadcasting in each market typically reach an audience, known as the ADI—Area of Dominant Influence—that extends far beyond the boundaries of any single local political jurisdiction. At the Seattle station where I worked our broadcasts reached as far north as the Canadian border and as far south as Vancouver, Washington, near Portland, Oregon. Were the station to broadcast a story about the Seattle mayor we instantly risked losing all those people who lived outside Seattle—the bulk of the audience. So instead the station focused on stories anybody anywhere could relate to: stories about fires, murders, and Keiko, the killer whale (aka: Free Willy). The reason local news all across the country looks and sounds the same and focuses on the same dreary stories—only the location seems to be different—is that research proves these are the only stories the masses will watch. And local TV remains a mass medium.

Despite the limits of TV, people say that it is the medium they trust most. Why? Because pictures are inherently compelling. If we see something on television, it happened. If we do not see it on television, it did not happen (unless someone talks about the event in a particularly dramatic way on television, in which case the event will seem to have happened on television). Think back to the events of the second half of the twentieth century and what comes to mind? Images: Martin Luther King's "I Have a Dream" speech, JFK's funeral, looters carrying away TV sets during the race riots of the 1960s, helicopters swooping down on rice paddies during the Vietnam War, Lyndon Johnson's prime-time announcement that he would not run for re-election, Neil Armstrong's walk on the moon, Nixon toasting Mao Zedong in China and boarding a helicopter following his resignation, Carter's malaise speech, the taking of American hostages in Iran, Reagan's demand in Berlin that Gorbachev "tear down this wall," the first Bush's "read my lips" promise, and Bill Clinton's claim that he "did not have sex with that woman."

In 1949, in a big spread in the *New York Times Magazine* devoted to television, Jack Gould noted, "A year ago the big question in television was: What is the future of the new medium? Today the question is: What is the future of those who look at television?" Today we have the answer. It's not what anyone would have hoped for.

It is worth pointing out that we have embarked on a radical experiment. How did it come about? Nobody deigned that it should happen. Nobody anticipated it would happen. Ours isn't the system dreamed up by the Founding Fathers. One imagines they would be quite horrified to find that the system they established in the eighteenth century has transmogrified into the one we have in the twenty-first. We don't really have a system at all. Ours is a non-system system. No one designed it. Like a bad highway wreck, it just happened.

Never in our history has the individual voter been at a greater disadvantage. He has been left to his own devices to figure out what he should think, where his interests lie, and how he should vote. At the very moment in history when we turned to the individual voter and said, here, you take the wheel of American democracy, we left him bereft of the help of the political party bosses, party machines, and labor unions, which in the past had helped shape his political understanding. Society even encouraged him to catch the news on television rather than reading it in a newspaper, though television is a far inferior transmitter of information.

It is hard to imagine anybody wanting things to develop as they have. Who would want a system in which the masses of voters would be left to determine the fate of the Republic on the basis of our television-based campaigns? Who would think to give the voters the kind of power they have now, knowing that their chief source of information about the candidates is the television spot? Who, knowing how complicated the world is today, would want voters to dictate the specific policies our politicians should follow given their general inability to handle complexity?

I imagine very few people would answer in the affirmative. But now, used to it as we are, we wouldn't have it any other way.

7

Our Dumb Politics:
The Big Picture

◆

Karl Rove deserves to be remembered as the man who
thought Americans should have enough education to
understand his fables but not enough to doubt them.
—ERIC RAUCHWAY IN *ALTERCATION* (AUGUST 14, 2007)

Decade by decade the American public has been getting
smarter and smarter—at least as measured by the number
of college degrees handed out at graduation. And decade
by decade our politics have been getting dumber and
dumber, owing to the forces I have singled out in earlier
chapters. How dumb?

Studies show that the speeches of presidents today are
pitched at the level of seventh graders; in the old days—
a scant half-century ago or so—they talked at the twelfth
grade level. Research also shows that young Americans

generally know far less about politics than their counterparts did a generation or two ago, even though they spend more time in school. What meager knowledge Americans do have about candidates' positions on the issues is picked up from those inane TV spots that proliferate at election time like a biblical plague of annoying locusts.

That our politicians no longer sound as intelligent as the Founding Fathers or Abraham Lincoln is taken for granted. But they no longer even measure up to the standard set by Millard Fillmore and Chet Arthur, neither of whom (1) ever publicly discussed his favorite underwear, (2) claimed that trees cause pollution, (3) charged that his opponents were "bozos," (4) said that "[t]he illiteracy level of our children are appalling," (5) cited his daughter's opinion about an issue of national importance in a political debate, (6) lifted up his shirt to show the press his big scar after surgery, (7) appeared on a tractor in a campaign ad to bolster his credentials as plain folk, (8) climbed into a tank to have his picture taken, (9) went on a show (such as Comedy Central's *The Daily Show*) to announce his candidacy for the presidency, (10) consulted an astrologer to decide when he should schedule a speech or a trip, (11) wore earth tones to increase his appeal to women, (12) appeared on a magazine cover smoking a giant cigar, (13) claimed that Jesus is his favorite philosopher in an obvious attempt to pander to religious voters, (14) took a poll to decide where he should vacation, or

(15) ever considered hiring a pollster, a media consultant, a speechwriter, or a spokesperson. And neither of them ever did a photo op.

Owing to the miracle of C-SPAN, one now can watch our solons in Washington D.C. as they declaim in the Senate. But who would want to? Judging from the wide-angle shots of the usually nearly empty floor, apparently not even other senators do. Except on rare occasions all that the members of the "world's greatest deliberative body" do now is drone. In our more democratic era there's not much of an audience for thoughtful speeches by an ordinary legislator, so the typical senator doesn't put in the effort required to deliver them. In Lincoln's day politicians could hold a crowd of thousands on the stump in thrall for hours. Today they practically have to dance a jig to catch our attention for even a few precious moments. One candidate for the U.S. Senate in 2006 was so desperate to attract notice in a crowded primary race that he ran a television spot that showed him literally jumping, fully clothed, into a lake. (He lost.)

I do not mean to imply that democracy in "the good old days" set a particularly high standard. No Golden Age of democracy existed in the past. And considering that until relatively recently most African-Americans could not even vote it would be offensive to make the claim. Nonetheless, it is helpful, I think, to point out the ways in which our present practices appear to disadvantage compared with what transpired in previous times.

When most of our early presidents needed to make a major speech they sat down and wrote it. This is unimaginable nowadays. Today it is not even clear that most of our modern presidents would know how to write a major speech if they had to. Not that we care. A pol can have trouble stringing ten words together on paper and nobody gives a hoot. But we do expect our presidents to have the fine sense of timing of a late-night comedian.

Along with his other many roles the modern president is our comedian-in-chief. Every year the president has to appear in a self-deprecating skit at the Gridiron Club dinner to show that he hasn't let power go to his head. To help him prepare, the president's speech-writing staff calls on the services of some local Washington joke writer. The next day the papers report how well the president performed. The reporters loved Bill Clinton's annual recitals. His monologue two months after the Lewinsky scandal broke—"So how was your week?" he deadpanned—may well have helped save his presidency by putting him back in the good graces of the Washington media establishment. Even First Ladies are invited to perform. Nancy Reagan appeared one year dressed in rags to poke fun at her love of fancy designer clothes. These appearances catch the mood of modern politics perfectly. It's no wonder the former actor Ronald Reagan told his biographer Edmund Morris that he sometimes wondered how anybody could succeed as a modern president if he hadn't been an actor. As Reagan told a group of students, "You'd be surprised how much being a good actor pays off [in politics]."

Gone are the days when a politician was simply a human being yearning for office. Today he is not a human being at all. He is a brand. Like a box of corn flakes he comes with slogans, a graphics package, and an ad campaign. Often he even has his own musical theme. By the end of a campaign when you hear his name you are expected to think of a rock and roll hit if you're a Democrat and a country melody if you're a Republican. The whole effort is designed in such a way that when you stroll into the voting booth on election day your head is filled with contrived images. Think of Bill Clinton and a picture of him playing his sax on the *Arsenio Hall Show* comes to mind. Think of George W. Bush and a picture of him standing around a barbecue with a bunch of good ol' boys pops into your head. Voting in these circumstances is no longer about issues; it's about feelings. Your feelings. Vote for Brand X and you can feel as secure as a soldier hunkered down in a Bradley tank. Vote for Brand Y and you can feel like a victorious Navy pilot who's just returned from a successful mission. All you have to do is pull the right lever. Did Hillary Clinton tear up on the eve of the New Hampshire primary? Well, then, she's human after all—let's vote for her!

At the time, just a half-century ago, that Ike appeared in the first thirty-second political spot, it was an unheard-of practice for a politician to submit to the kind of Madison

Avenue packaging required by television. Now the "Mad Men" are completely in charge. When a president gives a speech, they hook viewers up to a device that allows the researcher to measure every positive and negative twitch. The results are then rushed to the president's staff so they can learn how he has performed, which lines worked, and how they can best spin the results in his favor.

There have always been slogans in American politics, from even before the time of Tippecanoe and Tyler, too. George Washington was "first in war, first in peace, first in the hearts of his countrymen." During the war with the Barbary Pirates, Jeffersonians rallied around the cry "Millions for defense, but not one cent for tribute." But today a good slogan (or sound bite) is worth more to an aspiring politician than a chest full of war medals. Elections are often won and lost nowadays because a pol has had the good sense to hire an ad-man with the imagination to dream up a catchy slogan. Ronald Reagan may have won the presidency in 1980 in part because of a couple of witty lines scripted in advance of his single presidential debate with Jimmy Carter. "There you go again," Reagan said, with a slight grimace and the wisp of a smile. Then, in his closing comments, he asked Americans if they were better off now than they had been four years earlier—and that was that. Four years later, after the aging president turned in a mediocre performance in his first debate with the youngish Mondale, Reagan aides scrambled to figure out what had gone wrong. Reagan's wife Nancy knew. They had over-programmed her husband, stuffing his head so full of facts and figures he couldn't think straight. At the next debate Reagan had a one-liner ready to clear up the concern that he was too old for the job: "I will not make age an issue of this campaign. I am not going to exploit for political purposes my opponent's youth and inexperience." And *that* was that. Reagan himself believed that the debate "may have turned on only four words." Given the strength of the economy, Reagan undoubtedly would have won the 1984 election no matter what he said during this second debate, but his comment reassured Americans about the wisdom of re-electing him.

No one thing can explain the foolishness that marks so much of American politics. But what is striking is how often the most obvious cause—public ignorance—is blithely disregarded. Like the classic clue in many an Edgar Allan Poe mystery it remains hidden in plain sight.

Our reaction to radio talk show hosts who hunt for red-hot issues to make their caller boards light up is to castigate the hosts. Shouldn't the people listening to the claptrap also come in for their fair share of criticism? When Rush Limbaugh, who claims his talent is on loan from God, refers to liberal activist women as "feminazis" and when Don Imus lambastes blacks (such as Gwen Ifill, whom he referred to as the White House cleaning lady when she was the *New York Times* White House correspondent), should we not wonder about the common sense and simple grace of the people sitting in rapt attention at the receiving end of this foul-mouthed trash talk? (Several years of comments like his cleaning-lady "joke" finally got Imus fired, but his career was only temporarily derailed.)

Ask the man on the street who tunes in Rush and Imus why he listens to them, and you will probably hear that they are amusing. What exactly is amusing about pairing modern American women with the murderous felons of Hitler's dictatorship, the worst in history? What is funny about a thinly veiled racist allusion that brings to mind a black stereotype that as a society we have been trying to banish for at least two generations?

Now imagine for a moment that you are Karl Rove or any of the other high-flying political consultants who have shaped our public debates. What observation would you make about a nation with millions of listeners like these? Would you not reach the conclusion that they are a pretty crude bunch and that they are probably susceptible to pretty crude political appeals? Unless Rove believed it was his responsibility to raise the level of the voters— and I have yet to come across a single political consultant who thinks this way—he was apt to take them as they are and shape his campaigns accordingly.

You may be thinking to yourself that Rush's audience is mainly made up of "rednecks," and that, while they are a part of the broader public, they should not be considered representative. But who actually comprises Rush's audience of more than 20 million a week? According to a study conducted in 1996 by the University of Pennsylvania's An-

nenberg Public Policy Center, his listeners are better educated and "more knowledgeable about politics and social
issues" than the average voter. There are two ways of looking at this. Either we must reconsider our assessment of
Rush's show, conceding that it may be of a higher quality
than we were prepared to admit. Or we may have to reach
the unattractive conclusion that his audience is unrepresentative not because it is inferior in knowledge to the
larger pool of American voters but because it is superior.

If the latter is indeed the case, and I think it is, the wonder is not that American politics is conducted at its present infuriatingly low level but that on occasion it reaches
as high a level as it does.

In view of this situation one begins to understand that
what is wrong with our politics is worse than what many
people have been willing to concede. Our problem is not
with the cable news shows that in 2005 harped for months
on end about the tragic mysterious disappearance of a
beautiful young woman on a Caribbean island instead of
focusing on vital issues of more substance and broader
impact. Nor is our problem with the conniving politicians
in Washington D.C. who have hidden the impact of tax
cuts for the wealthy on our national budget by formally
sunsetting the cuts even as they prepare to extend them.
Nor: that we have too many demagogues. Rather, our
chief problem—or one of our chief problems—is that
which underlies all of these concerns: the limited capacity
of the general public.

Why do we have a sound-bite culture? Because in our mass democracy only issues rendered simple are susceptible to public debate. Any complicated idea perforce needs to be explained. As soon as you have to explain something in this country you have already lost most of the public. If an idea cannot be expressed on a bumper sticker you can probably give up any hope that it will ever attract much support. It likely will be ridiculed to death before it ever has a chance to be seriously considered. At the moment of its introduction somebody will be sure to cast aspersions on the intellectuals who dreamed it up in their ivory towers, and that will pretty much be the end of it.

Any measure of the American people should take into account more than their intelligence. Americans are often impressively generous, optimistic, and consistent (by this I mean that they do not swing wildly from one set of beliefs to another). And I am convinced that, if provided with the facts, ordinary Americans are perfectly capable of reaching a judicious conclusion unless some profound bias affects their thinking. (Of course, that's the rub: getting them the facts.) On occasion, relying on common sense, they stake out positions that put them ahead of their putative leaders. Polls in 2007 showed that the voters were in favor of higher gasoline mileage standards for automobiles to help curb pollution and reduce our dependence on foreign oil while the politicians, sensitive to the opposition of Detroit, opposed these policies.

But should the public be given credit for finally seeing a problem they had resolutely turned a blind eye to for decades? The only reason voters finally woke up was that gas prices had climbed dramatically, and gas prices are something everybody understands. You don't need a PhD to comprehend the impact of $3-a-gallon gas. Yet people still did not want to change their lifestyle. Give up their gas-guzzling SUVs? Fuhgetaboutit. Use mass transit? Fuhgetaboutit. In an interview on CBS, a driver in the Washington D.C. area said she wouldn't consider giving up her car to commute to work even if gas hit $4-a-gallon—though she lived across the street from a Metro stop and easily could make the switch. She loves her car too much, she said.

Psychiatrists have a word for this. It's called denial. It's an American disease. And there's no known cure.* Denial is not the same thing as unintelligence. Smart people are as susceptible to denial as others. But because of the way our political culture is organized, when the masses are guilty of denial it is very difficult for critics to stand up and point this out. And that's a sign of dumb politics. In a smart system, criticism would be welcome.

---

*But that doesn't mean we must give in to hopelessness. See Coda.

8

Our Mindless Debate
About 9/11

◆

Whenever war is declared, truth is the first casualty.

—Arthur Ponsonby in *Falsehood in Wartime:*
Propaganda Lies of the First World War (1928)

I would not wish to inflict on the reading public yet another long list of the many ways in which the Bush administration misled the country about 9/11, terrorism,
and the Iraq War. We have had enough such lists. I have
published many of them myself on the History News
Network, and at this point I don't want to read another
one. I have resolved not to add to the growing pile of
treatises on the subject until we gain access to the administration's private files, emails, diaries, and memoirs so we
can determine precisely what officials knew to be true and
what they knew to be false, and what they really hoped to

get out of the Iraq War. Whatever the particulars turn out to be, nothing in the misnamed "War on Terror" has gone as planned, not in Iraq or even in Afghanistan.

But much is to be gained from thinking about the public's response to the events of the last half-dozen years.

On the positive side, Americans did not make irrational demands of their leaders. American Muslims were not rounded up and sent to concentration camps after 9/11 (as Japanese-Americans were after Pearl Harbor). Mosques were not closed down. Nuclear weapons were not employed against our perceived enemies. And nobody was lynched. Given what has happened in American history any one of these responses or all of them might have been anticipated. That none occurred and that nothing like them occurred is worth noting.

But polls indicate that a significant segment of the American public was susceptible to wild conspiracy theories. A Scripps-Howard poll in 2006 found that 36 percent believe that it is "very likely" or "somewhat likely" that U.S. officials either allowed the attack to take place or were involved it.

Americans do not have a monopoly on conspiracy thinking. Nineteen percent of Germans said in a 2004 poll that 9/11 was the work of the CIA and Israel's Mossad. The French turned Thierry Meyssan's book *The Appalling Fraud* into a best-seller, despite the absence of evidence for its chief and crazy claim: that the Pentagon attacked itself on 9/11 with a cruise missile. Millions of

Muslims around the world persist in believing that Jews were given advance warning of the attack on the World Trade Center.

But instead of the thoughtful debate we should by rights have had in this country, we settled for slogans:

> *We must fight them over there so we don't have to fight them over here*
>
> *The Global War on Terror (GWOT)*
>
> *Mission Accomplished*
>
> *You are either with us or with the terrorists*
>
> *The axis of evil*

I myself am ready to declare a war on slogans, using "War on Slogans" as my slogan. I want the last slogan anybody ever uses to be my war on slogans. If we must have them, and I suppose we must, can we please stop slapping them on battleships and presidential sets? It is hard to remember now, but there once was a quaint time when presidents stood before empty backdrops and spoke to us, just plain damn spoke to us, without the help of a sea of helpful slogans behind them, in front of them, and to the side of them.

The slogans are symptomatic of our whole approach since 9/11. If ever there was a time when the public needed to hear a subject debated, and to hear all of it, the good, the bad, the ugly, and the confusing, that time was after 9/11. Instead, we asked shallow questions and settled for shallow answers.

On 9/11 itself, naturally enough, people expressed shock at the pictures on their television screens. But they also were shocked to learn that millions of people around the world hate us. I think that of the two great shocks of 9/11 the hatred of millions for America was possibly the more disturbing.

Of course, it *was* known that people hated us. Anybody who read the papers for the last thirty years and remembered what they read knew this. The war with Islamist terrorists did not begin on 9/11. Terrorists have been blowing up our buildings and airplanes and taking hostages for a generation, to the cheers of millions. In 1979 millions of Iranians whooped in joy at the taking of hostages at our embassy in Tehran. In 1981 Secretary of State Alexander Haig testified before the Senate that the number-one problem facing the United States was terrorism. But Americans did not remember this history.

Why *do* they hate us? About this we talked and talked and talked. But for all our talking we seldom seemed to get very far. In need of instant explanations we settled for a dubious mix of liberal and conservative platitudes: They hate us because they are poor. They hate us because they don't understand us. They hate us because they hate freedom.

It was always the ever-handy "They," although it was unclear to whom we were referring. Was it the whole

Muslim world or just Muslims in the Middle East? Or was it just a small subset of Muslims? There was a simplistic either-or dimension to the nomenclature that played on schoolyard fantasies that the world can be divided into good guys and bad guys (a common feature of the heavily mythologized American Western).

Myths drove our public debates. Religious conservatives in the mold of Jerry Falwell and Pat Robertson took a quite literal view of the myth of divine punishment, arguing that we got hit because God is mad at us for tolerating homosexuality and abortion. President Bush invoked another religious myth, the devil theory of history: Terrorists drove planes into our buildings because they are evil.

From the sidelines came demurrers. Political scientists pointed out that while many Muslims are poor (Afghanistan in 2001 ranked twelfth on the list of poorest countries in the world with an average annual income of $700 per capita), poverty by itself is not a cause of terrorism. Most poor people do not turn to terrorism. This should have been obvious to us but wasn't because the belief in poverty as a root cause of social problems is deeply embedded in the American consciousness. Confronted with 9/11, we acted on our first instinct, which was to filter events through the lens of our own experience. Although it was unlikely that the terrorists wanted from life what we want from it, we projected our own desires on them as if they did.

We assumed that Muslims around the world define *freedom* in the same way we do. They don't. According to a Gallup poll conducted in 2005, in eight Muslim-majority countries Muslim women do not believe that they are oppressed, however much we may think they are. Not one person out of the 8,000 whom Gallup interviewed volunteered that wearing a hijab or burqa, both of which are considered by many in the West to be symbols of the oppression of Muslim women, is either offensive or burdensome. Not in any of the countries where the interviews were conducted did a majority believe that the adoption of Western values would be helpful.

None of the popular explanations for 9/11, offered up in the initial response to the attacks, held up upon close inspection. But most Americans never seemed to get far beyond them, even though, in the years since, social scientists, historians, and other experts were busy developing far more comprehensive and subtle approaches. The historian Walter Laqueur developed evidence that fanatics are often inspired by a handful of charismatic leaders. Bernard Lewis, the doyen of Middle East Studies, explained that the rage the terrorists shared may have stemmed from the deep humiliation many Muslims in the Middle East feel, owing to their sense of having been bested by the West. The columnist Thomas Friedman, extending President Bush's simplistic analysis that the problem in the Middle East was the absence of democracy, explored the ways in which oil gives despotic leaders the opportunity to buy off their opposition without addressing the real needs of their people at large, leading to social stagnation and seething frustration. Others noted that democracy in the Middle East often meant in practice putting into power people who detest democracy, dooming the hopes of liberal reformers. And democracy, whatever its merits, is no guarantee against terrorism. The United States after all produced a Timothy McVeigh.

Ivan Eland, a political scientist with a libertarian bent, harped on the resentment many Muslims feel toward the United States for the way American power has been used for decades to control and crush them. As the journalist Stephen Kinzer, author of a history of governments the United States has overthrown, observed: "No one in the world cares how much or how little freedom there is in the United States. What angers them is the way the United States uses its power to crush freedom in other parts of the world."

Experts who examined the profiles of terrorists turned up evidence that Muslims from the Middle East who moved to Europe became susceptible to extremism after suffering from deep feelings of dislocation and alienation. Marc Sageman, a CIA case officer, reported that 70 percent of the 400 Islamist terrorists he studied committed themselves to violent jihad while living in a country other than the one in which they grew up. While abroad many became homesick and sought out friends at mosques, some of which became incubators of terrorism. Sageman's study in particular was useful in debunking the belief that terrorists turn to violence because they were neglected as children. He found that 90 percent came from caring families. Also surprising: Some 60 percent went on to college and more than 70 percent were married.

Historians who examined Osama bin Laden's career concluded it was unlikely he ordered the attack on the United States because of feelings of frustration growing out of a sense of powerlessness, as many believed. Actually, he was intoxicated with power. In his tendentious reading of history, it wasn't the Pope or Ronald Reagan who brought down the evil Soviet Empire but he who did so on the battlefields of Afghanistan. Having brought down one evil empire bin Laden now believed he could bring down another. And by bringing down America—the enemy from afar—he could bring down the American-dependent regimes he hated in the Middle East—the enemies that were near. This was a man with a plan. His resort to terrorism was no more an act of desperation than any leader's plan is. Rather, he was behaving very much as one would expect a billionaire's son would, using his money and power to rearrange the world to his own liking.

One explanation, which surfaced immediately after the attacks—that they represented an inevitable clash of civilizations—continued to obtain the support of some academics. But others noted that the inevitability of this clash was questionable. East and West are not monolithic.

In the nineteenth century and much of the twentieth, as European powers were carving up the Middle East, Muslims often looked to the United States as a source of inspiration. Arabs hated the French and the British, but not the Americans. In 1958 the Egyptian nationalist Gamal Abdel Nasser even celebrated the Fourth of July to show his warmth for the United States, which had condemned the British/French/Israeli plot to take over the Suez Canal, dooming it to failure.

As the United States geared up for a war against Iraq the shallowness of the public's understanding of Islam and history was exploited by the Bush administration. I do not wish to engage in a debate about the Iraq War. But the thought of planting a largely Christian army in the middle of the Muslim Middle East over the opposition of most countries in the region, when put as I have just put it, sounds daft. Why did it not ring bells of alarm to Americans in 2003 and after, especially as it became clear that our troops would be staying a long time and that no quick victory was possible? It did not because the administration saw to it that the issue was framed differently. We weren't planting an army. We were spreading God's miraculous gift of freedom to a benighted people very much in need of America's missionary help. It was another triumph of myth over logic.

Candor in the post–9/11 years has been conspicuous mainly by its absence. Only Richard Clarke, among public officials who were in charge at the time of the attack, has bravely admitted to error, confessing to a packed meeting of the 9/11 commission that he had personally let the country down. Had candor been in fashion the public debate would have included these other lines of inquiry: Why had The People elected to the presidency persons of both political parties wholly lacking in foreign policy experience, and not just once as in the case of George W. Bush, but over and over and over again? Why had The People taken so little interest in international issues that both their media and their leaders felt compelled through the years to limit public debate about foreign policy? Why did The People not pay attention to developments in Afghanistan and the Middle East? And why did they not remember the history of the Middle East—and their country's role in rearranging the affairs in that region's countries, putting in power tyrants such as the Shah and conniving to keep in power dictators like Saddam?

Even now, how many Americans know that in 1953 the CIA toppled the leader of the elected government of Iran, Mohammad Mossadegh, and replaced him with the Shah, which event led, some twenty-six years later, to the coup against the Shah in 1979, which in turn led to the establishment of a radical Islamist fundamentalist regime, which in turn inspired—and this is not too much of a stretch, I would aver—to the worldwide surge in fundamentalist politics that resulted in the attacks of September 11, 2001, as Stephen Kinzer contends in his fine book, *All the Shah's Men: An American Coup and the*

Roots of Middle East Terror? We may forget our own history; the Iranians most assuredly never do.*

We are now paying a terrible price for the public's indifference and superficiality. The question is: Will we learn from this debacle or ignore it?

---

*One wouldn't want to push this line of thinking too far. After all, it was Shiites who revolted against the Shah and Sunnis who backed bin Laden's attacks on the United States.

9

We Can't Even Talk About How Stupid We Are

◆

Hain't we got all the fools in town on our side? And
hain't that a big enough majority in any town?
— MARK TWAIN IN *HUCKLEBERRY FINN*

It is another of the curiosities of the last thirty or forty
years that, at just the moment that our politics were getting dumber, criticism of The People, who ostensibly are
in charge of our politics, largely vanished from public debate. Are they stupid? We mustn't say.

Many of us cannot *not* think it when we hear about surveys like the one showing that on the eve of the Iraq War
only one in seven Americans could find Iraq on the map.
But whether we live in Tuscaloosa or Tulsa, Portland,
Maine or Portland, Oregon, New York or Nevada,
whether we are in the top 1 percent of income earners or

in the bottom 20 percent with the day laborers, whether we hold a public position or toil in obscurity, whether we are Democrats or Republicans, we feel uncomfortable coming right out and saying publicly, The People sometimes seem awfully stupid.

Intimidating as the complexity of this subject is, as I have tried to show in previous chapters, it is not its complexity that deters people from considering it. It is our reluctance to confront our myths. And there are not many myths with which we are as reluctant to trifle as the one involved here, the myth of The People. Not only do we not dare speak publicly about The People's stupidity. We do not speak about the decision we have apparently taken as a society not to speak about the subject. Merely to raise the topic feels un-American.

Like the Victorians, whom we stigmatize for *their* hypocrisies, we have our own hypocritical ways of saying in public what is actually on our minds. One way of expressing our belief in the stupidity of The People is to talk about red staters or blue staters. We may say something like this: "Oh, the reason George W. Bush won in 2004 is that he was able to bamboozle all those red staters." By this we mean that the public—The People—dumbly allowed themselves to be manipulated into voting for Bush because he either played on their fears of another terrorist attack or exploited their sensitivities about gay marriage, abortion, or religion. Red staters or blue staters may be said to be in error, but The People? Not bloody often.

Only one columnist in our era dares to hint at it on a regular basis: the *New York Times*'s Thomas Friedman. He actually uses the word *stupid*. In March 2006 he came right out and said it:

> When it came to the Dubai ports issue, the facts never really had a chance—not in this political season. Still, it's hard to imagine a more ignorant, bogus, xenophobic, reckless debate than the one indulged in by both Republicans and Democrats around this question of whether an Arab-owned company might oversee loading and unloading services in some U.S. ports. If you had any doubts before, have none now: 9/11 has made us stupid.

By *us* Friedman did not mean the PhDs he hangs out with at the State Department or the *Times*. *Us* was code for The People.

Our reluctance to talk about The People honestly is odd on several levels. First, we speak in public without compunction about so much else, from the shape and angle of presidents' penises to the sexual identity of Hollywood movie stars. Second, there is abundant reason to think that millions of us believe that The People *are* stupid. In private we say so. We say it to our friends one on one and we say it to strangers encountered briefly on the bus. We say it on call-in radio shows, where our anonymity is assured, and we say it on blogs, which we consider public vehicles for the expression of private thoughts. But we do not say it on Fox News or *The Today Show* or the network evening news shows. Jon Stewart won't say it on his Comedy Central show. Nor will Michael Moore in his books or movies. (In his book *Stupid White Men*, Moore insists that the American people are *not* stupid.)

Some people may be made uncomfortable by the discussion of The People's limits and even find the exercise undemocratic. But raising questions about The People is not undemocratic. *Not* raising questions is. Asking questions is what democracy is all about. And one ought to be able in the twenty-first century—an age so thoroughly committed to the cause of democracy that everybody from the president of the United States down to the most heinous Middle East satrap seeks to persuade us they are its truest friend—to consider specific reservations about the way the members of a particular democracy are fulfilling their obligations without being suspected of antidemocratic heresies. To rule the inspection of our own democracy off-limits is both unreasonable and counterproductive. Are The People wise? We ought to be able to throw this question out for public debate. One can agree with Winston Churchill that democracy is the worst form of government except all the rest and still want to ask hard questions about it.

Most of the time when Americans hear a pol praise The People they feel complimented, not insulted. And on some level they believe that The People *are* wise and wonderful.

Americans love Hollywood's Jimmy Stewart as he rises to speak in the Senate in *Mr. Smith Goes to Washington.* They take genuine pride in the story of Abe Lincoln, the country bumpkin turned president.

Were the average American to stop and think about The People, it might occur to him that The People get a lot wrong. But ordinary Americans do not have the time or the inclination to think much about matters of this sort. Busy leading their lives in a 24/7 rat-race capitalistic culture—running to the store, earning a living, taking care of the kids—they do not have the luxury of reflection. Their inattentiveness is legendary.

Were pollsters to ask about the wisdom of The People, ordinary Americans might begin to reflect on the question. But voters are generally asked what they think about others, not what they think about themselves. They are rarely asked to grade themselves, to say how well they think they are fulfilling their democratic responsibilities. It is not in the interest of the politicians of either party or even the media to ask:

Do you strongly agree or strongly disagree with the following statements:

1. The People are paying attention to world events.

2. The People are foolishly so absorbed in their own lives that they have no idea what is happening in foreign countries.

3. The People are well-schooled in the domestic issues
   facing the country.

One can hear the ordinary American answering (as the
pollster scampers away), *Say Mack, I believe in The People.
I believe in the flag, God, and country, too. You got a problem
with that?* *

If you are a Baby Boomer you may be thinking that the
reluctance to criticize The People in public is not strange
at all. That's just the way things are. During the adult
years of the Baby Boomers that *is* mainly the way things
have been. But that is not how things have always been. A
remarkable change has taken place in our society in the
last generation or two, though we have not stopped to an-
alyze it. We should.

Running through American history one detects, until
recently, a constant tension between faith in The People
and contempt for them. This tension was most evident at
the time of the Founding Fathers, who fretted endlessly
about the virtue of The People, whether virtue was
needed, and the ways in which democratic passions could
be blocked and channeled. The design of the Constitu-

---

*We do ask what people know about various subjects, but this is differ-
ent from asking them to grade themselves. One poll that did so found in
1988 that 35 percent believe that "voters" do not make much of an attempt "to find out about the candidates." See Gil Troy, *See How They Ran:
The Changing Role of the Presidential Candidate* (Harvard University Press,
1996), p. 274.

tion reflects this tension. It opens with a broad and generous statement, "We the people." But by paragraph two there's the hint that The People may not quite be up to the task of self-government. Only the lower half of the Congress was to be popularly elected. The Senate was to be selected by the state legislatures. The president was to be selected by an Electoral College. And federal judges and Supreme Court justices were to be appointed by the president and confirmed by the Senate. In other words, only one-half of one branch of the federal government was to be directly accountable to The People.

It is often said that the drafters of the Constitution were most concerned with creating a strong central government. What is seldom said, as the historian Forrest McDonald points out in *Novus Ordo Seclorum: The Intellectual Origins of the Constitution*, is that one of their motivations in replacing the weak Articles of Confederation with the Constitution was that they wished to curb the power of the state governments, several of which had come to be dominated by powerful demagogues: Patrick Henry in Virginia, John Hancock in Massachusetts, and Samuel Chase in Maryland. No republic in history had survived for long. And here, just a few short years after the Revolution, was evidence that, in our own, The People were becoming attached to rulers who played on their emotions.

A great fear expressed by the founders was that ordinary people would use their power at the ballot box to confiscate the wealth of the many and give it to the few, as was already happening in several states, where creditors were on the defensive. To forestall this possibility the founders sought to turn elections into contests over character. In an election in which the character of the candidates was primary, people of refinement would likely be selected to rule. To our surprise perhaps the last thing the founders wanted was that elections would be fought over issues. Under those circumstances it was feared that the chief issue every time would be how the many could steal the wealth of the few.

Reading their commentaries today one senses that many of the founders were so desperate to find reasons to believe in The People that they were willing to grasp at any argument they came across. One of the strangest they readily adopted was the philosopher David Hume's belief in inertia. The People, believed Hume, could be trusted with power because they would be inclined to leave things well enough alone unless pushed by extraordinary circumstances to embrace change. Hume's analysis was astute. Americans generally are conservative (meaning, they oppose change). But it was hardly a resounding argument in favor of popular rule. It amounted to saying The People could be trusted not because they are trustworthy but because they are basically passive.

It is a measure of the great distance we have traveled since the Revolution that no politician today could utter comments regularly heard in the public debates involving the founders. Who today could say, along with George Mason, "It would be as unnatural to refer the choice of a proper magistrate to the people as it would to refer the choice of colors to a blind man"? Certainly no politician could repeat the arguments of Alexander Hamilton at the Constitutional Convention without disavowing them shortly after with the excuse that they had been drinking. That we have checks on The People is accepted; no one argues in favor of abolishing the Senate, for instance. But the reason these checks are needed is seldom spelled out. For to spell out the reasons, as Adams did in the passage quoted below, is to say that which in modern American politics is unsayable:

> We may appeal to every page of history we have hitherto turned over, for proofs irrefragable, that the people, when they have been unchecked, have been as unjust, tyrannical, brutal, barbarous and cruel as any king or senate possessed of uncontrollable power. The majority has eternally and without one exception usurped the rights of the minority.
>
> All projects of government, formed upon a supposition of continual vigilance, sagacity, and virtue, firmness of the people, when possessed of the exercise of supreme power, are cheats and delusions.

To our ears Adams's words sound—to appropriate a word from religion that seems particularly apt in the context—blasphemous. Our civil religion forbids such language. We may in the privacy of our own homes think such thoughts when The People act in ways contrary to our wishes. When our side loses in an election we may want to throw a shoe at the television set as we bemoan our fate to have been born in a country where The People are so stupid as to have elected So-and-So. But there is in us a timidity that stops us from acknowledging such thoughts in public.

More soothing were the panegyrics of James Madison and Thomas Jefferson, both of whom expressed a typical eighteenth-century republican's confidence in the ability of ordinary (white) men to make moral choices if given the opportunity, though I could cite quotations from the early Madison that would sound very Hamiltonian. And even Jefferson decried the despotism of the state legislatures, expressing his conviction in one notable letter that there was as great a danger from 173 despots as from 1. Why, given their reservations, did they have confidence things would turn out right? It was in part because of their faith in the Constitution and their belief that it would be "a machine that would go of itself." The phrase belongs to James Russell Lowell, a figure of the late nineteenth century. But it well expressed the views of the founders, who thought of the Constitution as a machine that would keep the Republic on track no matter whom the damn fool voters might elect. By the time Jefferson died in 1826 the Constitution had become the bedrock of the Republic, but by then he had begun to worry more than he ever had earlier about the wisdom of ordinary voters. He had predicted that within a generation everybody in America would be a Unitarian. Instead, sectarianism had grown—an alarming development to a man like Jefferson, who associated religion with superstition. Furthermore, Andrew Jackson, whom Jefferson considered unfit to be president, was well on his way to the White House. This was progress? A kind of reverse Darwinism had taken place.

Liberals have always been reluctant to challenge the myth of The People. To the liberal the blame for our various troubles can almost always be laid at the feet of some bogeymen at the top: the barons of Wall Street, the titans of big business, the lobbyists on Capitol Hill, who are said to wield power over the rest of us in secret and often deleterious ways.

The liberal's approach is brilliant politics. It leaves The People off the hook whenever bad things happen. But as the basis of a philosophy it is flawed. For The People often are to blame for American failures. A weakness of liberalism is that the ideology leaves liberals unable to account for the hard realities encountered in the real world. When Walter Lippmann discovered that The People could easily be manipulated by propaganda he found himself at sea ideologically. Nothing in liberalism could explain The People's misguided behavior and nothing in liberalism suggested a fix. New York Governor Alfred E. Smith's bromide that all the ills of democracy can be cured by more democracy sounded good but provided little guidance. Liberal intellectuals have struggled with the contradictions. Evidence that the Populists were anti-Semitic pushed liberal historian Richard Hofstadter to the uncomfortable conclusion that even reformers committed to a progressive agenda could be seriously flawed. In tracing the history of the anti-intellectualism that so marked the movement of Goldwater conservatism in the 1960s, Hofstadter came around to the disturbing conclusion that its roots lay in good old Jacksonianism, the foundation stone of modern liberalism. It was Jacksonians after all who distrusted expertise.

In the modern era liberals have continued to claim that they are optimistic about The People. But three developments in the last half-century have conspired to undermine their faith. First was the reaction to the Civil Rights Movement, which laid bare the racist beliefs of thunderous majorities of white Southerners. Second was the decline in popularity of the Great Society, which came as a shock. Third, and finally, was the pattern of lost elections. As conservatives won election after election liberals began to doubt the good sense of the voters. How could a country that had elected Franklin Delano Roosevelt and Harry Truman and rejected Barry Goldwater have become a country that elected Ronald Reagan and the two Bushes?

In a search for answers some Democrats turned inward and asked if the party had made mistakes. The so-called Atari liberals—Gary Hart, Michael Dukakis, and Bill

Bradley—contended that the party had been punished for inflexibility, for remaining wedded to New Deal big-government solutions at a time when the economy was becoming postindustrial and global. Centrists like Al From, founder of the Democratic Leadership Council, argued that the party had gone too far left, leaving its natural working-class supporters, particularly Catholics, alienated. Still others, such as Ralph Nader, insisted that the Democrats had surrendered to the corporations, erasing any meaningful difference between them and the Republicans.

One obvious factor in the liberals' decline was their embrace of the Civil Rights Movement and the women's movement. To put this candidly: Voters punished liberals at the polls not necessarily because of what they had done wrong but for what they'd done right. This rankled. Being punished for their support of out-of-date policies was one thing. But finding that the voters were unforgiving about the liberals' forthright stands taken on issues of conscience was hard to fathom. For it put liberals at odds with their own belief in The People. Caught in the contradictions of their own ideology—their love of The People and The People's seemingly misguided rejection of them at the polls—they turned angry. They remain angry.

Like Paddy Chayefsky's Howard Beale, Democrats don't want to take it anymore. They're mad as hell. They want to open the windows and SCREAM! It's no wonder they elected their own Howard—Howard "I Have a

Scream Speech" Dean—as party chairman after the 2004 debacle. Dean, say what you will about him, knows how to shake the rafters.

Democrats are angry for a multitude of reasons. They are angry that Bill Clinton did not seem to get more done. They are angry that when he got into political trouble he turned repeatedly to Republicans like David Gergen and Dick Morris for guidance. They are angry that Clinton had sex with an intern and lied about it. They are angry that Kenneth Starr went after Clinton relentlessly and humiliated him. They are angry that liberal-bashing became a national pastime, turning books demonizing liberals into *New York Times* best-sellers. Democrats are so angry they are willing to admit that there are American politicians they actually hate. They hate Newt Gingrich. They hate Zell "Spitball" Miller, the turncoat Georgia Democrat. And of course they hate George W. Bush.

Because they are angry they cannot see what is really bothering them. It is not just the typical "loser's lament" (to borrow the historian Gil Troy's nice phrase). The cause of their discontent goes deeper. It has to do with the striking dissonance between what America has been for years and what America previously seemed to be. Once the United States seemed to be a liberal country open to liberal ideas. Until the 2006 elections it was beginning to seem like a conservative country openly hostile to liberalism.

It would have been helpful to Democrats to hold an honest conversation about the real sources of their discontent. But they couldn't without facing foursquare the myth of The People. So instead they entertained a series of excuses for their electoral failures, only some of which even came close to the truth.

The comforting answer many liberals came up with was that, time and again, nefarious forces had bamboozled people. Nixon did it by appealing to the stark grievances of whites who felt threatened by the new breaks given African-Americans. Reagan did it by combining a sunny personality with manipulative media campaigns. George W. Bush did it by exploiting people's fears about 9/11.

In book after book liberals decried the many ways in which they had been victimized by Republicans. George Lakoff, in *Don't Think of an Elephant*, charged that Republicans had manipulated language to fool the voters, substituting, for instance, the phrase *death tax* for *estate tax*. Al Gore argued that what was wrong was that Republicans had replaced reason with emotion in public debates, putting Democrats at a disadvantage. Drew Westen, a social scientist, argued that the problem was that Democrats weren't emotional enough and recommended that they adopt the same manipulative tactics Republicans had used to great success. Still others charged that right-wing radio talk show hosts had inflamed public opinion with demagogic appeals.

One of the largely unspoken assumptions of these liberal analyses was that people are easily duped. But few pundits admitted this, placing the emphasis, once again, on the nefarious manipulators. Even the liberal journalist Thomas Frank, whose best-seller *What's the Matter with Kansas?* recounted the self-destructive votes he believed his fellow Kansans cast in succeeding elections owing to the Republicans' clever use of social issues like abortion and homosexuality, in the end attributed the voters' misguided support for Republicans to a "manipulative ruling class" not unlike that which lords over the masses in much of the Arab Middle East. As a good liberal he simply could not hold the voters themselves ultimately responsible.*

Fully in the grip of the myth of The People, some liberals insist that but for the manipulation of dastardly Republicans and powerful special interests Americans would support Democrats most of the time because basically Americans really are liberal. Eric Alterman, a historian and pundit, cites polls showing that 65 percent of Americans favor guaranteed health insurance and 77 percent favor doing whatever is necessary to protect the environment. The thought that Americans might have strong

---

*Did Kansans in fact vote Republican because they were manipulated? I very much doubt it. I suspect they voted Republican because they are inherently conservative and Republicans were better able than Democrats to tap into those feelings. Frank takes it as axiomatic that nobody in his right mind could vote time and again for Republicans on the basis of social issues, though why this is so is never made clear. Why should social issues be given a lower priority than economic issues? If giving gays rights can be important to Democrats, ending abortions, it should follow, can be important to Republicans. And while Republicans failed to overturn *Roe v. Wade*, they were able over the years to place restrictions on abortion, giving the voters some of what they wanted.

conservative impulses cannot be abided. The People must always be assumed to be liberal at heart since liberalism celebrates The People. And round and round we go, using this logic, in an unending cycle of self-delusion.

Alterman at least admits that The People for many years did not support Democrats. The pollster Stanley Greenberg remains convinced that they did. The Democratic Party's losing streak? What losing streak? "But for the butterfly ballots in Florida or Ralph Nader or Clinton's moral lapses or Al Gore's conceit few observers doubt that the Democrats would have won the presidency three times in a row, a feat equaled only by Reagan and Bush in this half century."

Other liberals make the argument that while Americans talk conservative they are operationally liberal. That is, they like to think that they prefer small government and low taxes while actually favoring big-government programs like Social Security and Medicare that require the imposition of big-government taxes. I believe that this argument has merit. The liberal delusion is to draw the false conclusion that in their hearts voters are therefore really liberal. Actually, they are what they are: both conservative and liberal. As long as Republicans don't tamper with the programs Americans like, there's no reason for Americans to vote for Democrats. (George W. Bush's plan to revamp Social Security called into question the Republicans' support for the traditional big-government programs Americans like. It got nowhere.)

Bush's victory in 2004 was sobering and more than many liberals could stomach, prompting a new round of hand-wringing. So disturbing was his re-election that some Democrats finally began to wonder about the intelligence of the voter. The billionaire George Soros came right out and said he believed that The People are stupid. From time to time the historian Arthur Schlesinger, Jr., indicated he agreed. As the war in Iraq dragged on into its fifth year Frank Rich, the *New York Times* columnist, finally admitted that although he had "always maintained that the American public was the least culpable of the players during the run-up to Iraq" it was now "hard to give Americans en masse a pass. We are too slow to notice, let alone protest, the calamities that have followed the original sin." But there wasn't much talk like that. And with victory in the 2006 midterm elections Democrats began to hope that The People were with them again. If anyone was going to pursue the line of thinking Soros and the others opened up it wasn't going to be liberals.

That left conservatives to take up the challenge. Might they begin questioning The People? Until the modern era they readily admitted that The People are untrustworthy and ignorant.

The conservatives' faith in free markets was based, in part, on their fear of democracy. In an echo of the concerns of the Founding Fathers, who of course never embraced democracy, they worried that voters would use their power at the ballot box to soak the rich to finance

socialistic schemes. They therefore firmly attached themselves to free-market capitalism once the masses got the
vote, in the belief that the dividing up of the resources of
the country was better left to the market rather than to
the whims of the voters. Their embrace of capitalism was
sometimes awkward, given that capitalism is an engine of
change and conservatives, by definition, were leery of
change. And often corporations, in the pursuit of profits,
seemed to undermine the traditional values conservatives
were trying to preserve. Nonetheless, the union of conservatives and capitalists flourished. Fear of The People
was the powerful cement.

In his path-breaking history of conservatism, written
in the 1950s, Clinton Rossiter began his definition of the
Right with the statement that it is "skeptical of popular
government." Today books barely even mention that this
skepticism was once a prominent feature of conservatism.
One of the finest histories of modern conservatism is *The
Right Nation*, by John Micklethwait and Adrian
Wooldridge. On page 46 there's a brief reference to Albert Jay Nock, a prominent conservative thinker from
the pre-war period who "looked down on the common
people." But that is the last we hear of Nock or of
thinkers like him, save for a few Straussians (students
of an academic named Leo Strauss). The main parade of
conservatives who figure in the rest of the book—starting
with Richard Nixon, son of a failed small businessman—
celebrate the common people. In short, "Nixon's genius

was to pick up on George Wallace's insurgency in the Democratic Party and direct populism against cultural elites: against what Nixon saw as the effete snobs who controlled institutions like Harvard and the *Washington Post*."

Skepticism of popular government grew naturally out of the bedrock conviction that man is fundamentally depraved, sin is universal, and redemption is rare. So essential were all of these beliefs to conservatism that one is hard-pressed to imagine what is left of a conservatism that exists without them. To read Rossiter is to realize just how far we have come from the classic definition:

No truth about human nature and capabilities, the Conservative says, is more important than this: man can govern himself, but there is no certainty that he will; free government is possible but far from inevitable. Man will need all the help he can get from education, religion, tradition, and institutions if he is to enjoy even a limited success in his experiments in self-government. He must be counseled, encouraged, informed, and checked. Above all, he must realize that the collective wisdom of the community, itself the union of countless partial and imperfect wisdoms like his own, is alone equal to the mightiest of social tasks. A clear recognition of man's conditional capacity for ruling himself and others is the first requisite of constitution-making.

Can it really be that conservatism has changed that much? The answer is that it has, but most of us do not realize it and conservatives do not wish us to.

Formerly, hard-headed critiques of democracy were ubiquitous in conservative thought. The trouble with conservatives was not that they were reticent with their views on the subject but that they were downright voluble. You could not shut them up. There is not enough room in this chapter to conduct a thorough review of the critiques conservatives advanced, but neither is one necessary. Just think of the great conservative voices of the latter half of the nineteenth century and the first half of the twentieth. Can you name one who celebrated The People (being careful to exclude the remarks made by the craven politician in the course of a stump speech)? I cannot unless it be the Oklahoman Willmoore Kendall, who professed great faith in the virtuousness of ordinary Americans. And even Kendall argued that the only way to make sure that The People remain virtuous was to see to it that they deferred to a "select minority" who serve as moral teachers and custodians of the culture. Conservatives on the whole were too busy worrying about the failures of American democracy to say anything positive about The People. Driven to pessimism by their fears of the collectivist tendencies of modern politics, they could not, even with the victory of the Allies in World War II, find much to celebrate.

A sampling of quotes from three conservative thinkers of the past century is illustrative:

- H. L. Mencken: "Democracy is the theory that holds that the common people know what they want, and deserve to get it good and hard."

- William F. Buckley, Jr.: "The commitment by liberals to democracy has proved obsessive, even fetishistic. It is part of their larger absorption in Method, and Method is the fleshpot of those who live in metaphysical deserts. . . . The democracy of universal suffrage is not a bad form of government; it is simply not necessarily nor inevitably a good form of government."

- Albert Jay Nock: "[T]here must be as many different kinds of democracy in this country as there are of Baptists. Every time one of our first-string publicists opens his mouth, a 'democracy' falls out; and every time he shuts it, he bites one in two that was trying to get out."

Conservatives did not entirely abandon their suspicions of The People in the modern era. The old warhorses of the movement stayed on the anti-democratic bridle path they had trod earlier. As a student in high school I attended a week-long summer seminar at Bryn Mawr in the early 1970s sponsored by the right-wing Intercollegiate Studies Institute at which I was tutored in the precepts of Russell Kirk, Leo Strauss, and other conservative intellectuals who were openly hostile to the direction of American democracy. I recall clearly the teenager's thrill that I was a member of a group that fearlessly dared challenge the taboos of conventional thinking. My chief attraction to conservatism was that at the time it seemed a lot more radical and interesting than liberalism. Pessimism fascinated; it was entirely outside the experience of a kid raised in the suburbs of New Jersey as I was. I eagerly awaited the new issues of *Modern Age* and the *Intercollegiate Review*—two of the movement's chief intellectual vehicles—which struck defiant notes of iconoclasm.*

I, however, was in the minority. Most Americans prefer optimism. For the conservatives to have a prayer of political success, they had to forsake the pessimism to which they had long been devoted. Conversion proved to be far easier than anyone might have expected. As the liberal order began to collapse (which conservatives had long predicted), conservatives began winning popular support. The worse things got—as more and more cities went up in flames, as more kids died in Vietnam, as crime rates

---

*I remained under the spell of conservatism until Watergate, at which point I threw down my pitchfork in disgust and reconciled myself to the liberal persuasion of my parents.

soared—the more likely it was that The People would move right. Soon victory followed victory.

It is hard now, after decades of conservative dominance, to realize just how unexpected a development this was. For years conservative victory had seemed the dream of fantasists. "We shall tax and tax, and spend and spend, and elect and elect," FDR's aide Harry Hopkins allegedly bragged. And for years, that was precisely the formula Democrats followed with great success. Upon its debut in 1955 *National Review*, the conservative weekly begun by William F. Buckley, Jr., acknowledged the conservatives' isolation: "*National Review* is out of place, in the sense that the United Nations and the League of Women Voters and the *New York Times* and Henry Steele Commager are in place. It is out of place because, in its maturity, literate America rejected conservatism in favor of radical social experimentation."

But by the mid–1960s conservatives could argue convincingly that the liberal promises were wreaking havoc. Columbia University's Martin Anderson demonstrated in *The Federal Bulldozer* that urban renewal was a practical failure and morally obscene: To make room for 28,000 new homes the government had destroyed 126,000 existing homes (between 1949 and 1962). Other conservatives took note of the failures of trust-busting, the welfare system, and desegregation. Even liberals began to recognize that the policies they had put in place were failing to bring into existence the new world they had promised. Daniel Patrick Moynihan, the liberal Harvard sociologist, famously recommended that blacks would for a time benefit from a period of "benign neglect."

Face to face with these failures, the liberal reeled and the conservative hooted in joy. Just four years after the collapse of Barry Goldwater's campaign Richard Nixon was elected president of the United States. Conservatism survived even Watergate. Under the circumstances it was difficult for all but splenetic conservatives to continue writing tracts about the decline of the West, the absence of wisdom in The People, or the crack-up of democracy. For once The People seemed amenable to the conservative vision. Democracy seemed to work.

A visitor from the New Deal dropping in on America in 1969 might have wondered if the world had not turned upside down. Now it was conservatives like Richard Nixon, instead of liberals, who were demonizing elitists and celebrating the Silent Majority. After Nixon came Ronald Reagan, whose effusiveness for the common man made him sound like his one-time political hero, Franklin D. Roosevelt. As John Patrick Diggins, a Reagan biographer, astutely observes, the Founding Fathers believed that "the people are the problem and government the solution" while Reagan convinced us that the people are virtuous and that government's the problem. "It worked," Diggins notes. "Reagan never lost an election."

In the twenty-first century conservatives have joined liberals in competing as flatterers of the vox populi. Whatever The People believe is right. On Fox News nary a single commentator is given time to express skepticism of The People. In their hurry to curry favor with viewers Fox News conservatives are unwilling to suggest that the voters are ever in error. It is never the voters who make mistakes. It is liberals. We are all populists now.

The timing of this development could not be stranger. Here we are in the Second Gilded Age, when every single person on the Forbes 400 list is a billionaire, and CEOs often earn several times more money in a day than their employees do in a year, and the conservatives who are the defenders of wealth and privilege are claiming to be one with The People while liberals are derided as elitists. As the saying goes, *Only in America!*

What sustains the conservative faith in The People is, above all, the resistance of millions of ordinary voters to the social changes that have taken place in modern American life involving abortion, homosexuality, and feminism. So long as these voters persist in their resistance, conservatism will remain a powerful force. If fresh challenges to the social order are made, conservatism undoubtedly will enjoy a rebirth.

For now, conservatism seems on the wane. Liberals, who haven't had a great year since 1965, seem poised to take over all three branches of the federal government in

2008. The economist and liberal columnist Paul Krugman is convinced that the dawn of a new liberal era is
upon us. If it is, one can be certain that liberals will stop
complaining about The People.

Will conservatives start to do so? My guess is they will.
Already there have been signs that conservatives are beginning to doubt that Americans merit the confidence
leaders like Reagan expressed in them. After President
Bill Clinton's acquittal in the Senate impeachment trial
Paul Weyrich, a long-time conservative activist who
helped found the Heritage Foundation, expressed his
doubts in "An Open Letter to Conservatives":

> Cultural Marxism is succeeding in its war against our culture.
> The question becomes, if we are unable to escape the cultural
> disintegration that is gripping society, then what hope can we
> have? Let me be perfectly frank about it. If there really were
> a moral majority out there, Bill Clinton would have been dri-
> ven out of office months ago. It is not only the lack of politi-
> cal will on the part of Republicans, although that is part of
> the problem. More powerful is the fact that what Americans
> would have found absolutely intolerable only a few years ago,
> a majority now not only tolerates but celebrates. Americans
> have adopted, in large measure, the MTV culture that we so
> valiantly opposed just a few years ago, and it has permeated
> the thinking of all but those who have separated themselves
> from the contemporary culture.

> ... I no longer believe that there is a moral majority. I
> do not believe that a majority of Americans actually shares
> our values.

At present most conservative leaders have stifled their desire to lambaste the public. As long as the possibility of
cultural retrenchment remains possible they'll remain
hopeful—and will continue to say nice things about The
People.

Thus do we find ourselves where we are today—in the
pitiful position that neither liberals nor conservatives are
prepared to say to The People: Stop and pay attention.
Liberals *cannot* because their ideology leaves them unprepared to find fault with The People. Conservatives *have
not* because The People repeatedly put them in power. In
other words: Neither liberals nor conservatives have had
anything meaningful to say about The People's failure
over the last few years to grapple with complexity, misinformation, and fear.

What it means in a democracy to have so few understand how our government works, who pays taxes, and
how they are spent we do not care to inquire about too
deeply. If we did, what troublesome debates we would
have to have. We would have to consider the possibility
that polls are meaningless since the polled often lack a
sound basis upon which to make their choices. We would
have to question the use of referendums and initiatives.
We would have to consider requiring voters to pass a

basic civics test before allowing them to cast a ballot. We might have to discuss the repeal of the Seventeenth Amendment in order to allow state legislatures to choose the members of the U.S. Senate as they used to. We might have to consider allowing the Electoral College to actually make the real decision in electing presidents as Alexander Hamilton wanted. And we would have to say to the politicians who insist on telling us The People are wise and true that they are full of it and should cease forthwith from insulting our intelligence with empty democratic gestures.

Coda: Hope

◆

Do not be too severe upon the errors of the people, but
reclaim them by enlightening them.
— THOMAS JEFFERSON

At a public gathering two years before he died Arthur
Schlesinger, Jr., the esteemed historian, confessed that
contemporary politics made him depressed. After running
through a litany of grievous mistakes made by Mr. Bush
and the public's acquiescence in them, he observed that
our democracy is only some 200 years old and asked:
What makes us think it is permanent?

Good question.

Given all that we know, should we be hopeful it is?
Reason is under assault everywhere one turns. Each election campaign seems worse than the last. Myths are ubiquitous. Nearly half of the eligible voters don't vote and
many of those who do don't seem to know what they're

voting for. As the debunker Bergen Evans observed a half-century ago, "ideas of the Stone Age exist side by side with the latest scientific thought." Stupidity is common and brains, common sense, and courage are rare.

And yet not all is grim. In a country as rich and powerful as ours stupid decisions only on occasion have cataclysmic consequences. Even when they do, as with Katrina, which cost the lives of some 2,000 people, or in Iraq, where tens of thousands have perished, it is unlikely that stupidity will seriously put in jeopardy the survival of our Republic. So we muddle through.

For those who live on hope—and don't we all—several developments of the last decade or so are promising.

I find the Internet promising.

I find blogging promising.

Where they may lead is anybody's guess. But one can hope that they will give the intelligent the tools needed to take political campaigns to a higher level rather than merely empowering, as sometimes currently seems the case, nitwits, extremists, and the obnoxious.

It is even possible that television will finally fulfill the hopes of its inventors. Until the 1990s hardly any Americans cared about deficit reduction. The conservatives who were supposed to care no longer did after their hero, Ronald Reagan, tripled the national debt. But then in the spring of 1992 the billionaire Ross Perot decided that the national debt was a national disgrace and that somebody had to do something about it and that this somebody would be him. He announced on *Larry King Live* that he was running for president. Old Washington hands didn't know what to make of his campaign. Ed Rollins came on board and was appalled to discover that Perot had no staff to speak of, no position papers, and no field offices. The campaign consisted of Ross Perot's media appearances and little else. Using his own money, some $60 million, Perot bought several thirty-minute blocks during prime time to talk about various issues. He devoted one entire show to the deficit, using nothing more than comically low-tech pie charts and graphs to help make his points. Media critics predicted the shows would be a ratings disaster. They actually attracted an enormous audience, one show even outdrawing the baseball playoffs. Perot succeeded in focusing the country's attention on deficits—and forcing the other candidates in the race, Bill Clinton and George H. W. Bush, to share his concern. A Lou Harris poll found that 73 percent of viewers were impressed with the infomercials; 34 percent said they were "very effective." Perot may have failed to ride the popularity of his shows into the White House, but he helped create a constituency for deficit reduction that Clinton found helpful when he decided it was essential to address the problem. Taxes were increased, the deficit came down, and the economy roared. (No lessons in politics are permanent; we have now gone back to deficit spending, of course.)

No candidate since Perot has seen fit to replicate his simple use of television. But maybe someone will. Maybe

Al Gore will get some billionaire to put him and his global warming slide show on television in prime time so even more Americans can learn about the environmental threats we face. (I myself wasn't wholly convinced of our dire situation until watching his presentation.)

But if we want real change we will have to confront the story of The People's failures I outline in this book.

Nothing I have said should be taken to imply that I believe that the fault, dear Brutus, lies solely in ourselves. Our institutions have failed us and so have our elites. A century of experience with mass politics in a mass media world shows that nobody can be trusted with power: not the voters, who have proven themselves susceptible to propaganda; not the elites, whom Walter Lippmann hoped would guide public opinion; and certainly not the media or our political institutions. James Madison was right. All must check and balance all.

How then shall we proceed?

The first step is to start speaking honestly about the limitations of public opinion. What might a genuine critique encompass? I should think it would include these questions among others: Does it make sense to trust the masses with power if they derive their opinions, as Virginia Wolfe complained, from "things written in chalk and large and repeated over and over again"? Are ordinary people capable of reaching sound decisions if propaganda can be used to great effect to shape their views? Does the modern media produce such an overload of information that ordinary voters feel anxious and alienated, leaving them vulnerable to simplistic appeals?

S. I. Hayakawa, the semanticist, raised two questions that might form the basis of a sustained critique relevant to our times. In *Language in Action*, he explores the appeal of propaganda, asking why and how it works. He argues that demagogues succeed in persuading people to support one thing or another through the use of meaningless abstractions, words like *freedom* and *liberty*. To guard themselves against the emotional power of such words, citizens need to be taught to demand language that is concrete. If an abstract word is used in a speech with no meaningful referent, the listener should disregard it. If the word *freedom* is not defined precisely, it should be ignored.

A second of his observations deals with a subject that is especially resonant. It is the use by demagogues of what he calls the "two-valued orientation." By this he means the false division of the world into two categories, good and evil. Anything that stands in the way of the demagogue's goals is considered evil, anything that furthers his goals is considered good. There is no middle ground. The consequence of this Manichean approach to politics is that the resort to violence is more likely. To compromise is to give in to the demands of the devil. "As in Germany," he wrote, "it produces here the results of intoxication, fanaticism, and brutality. . . . Listeners who uncritically permit themselves to be carried away by such oratory week after week almost invariably find their pulses rising, their fists clenching, and the desire to act violently accumulating within them."

I do not know if Hayakawa would have opposed the Iraq War. But I am confident he would have been appalled at the way it was successfully sold. If we "think like savages and babble like idiots, we all share the guilt for the mess in which human society finds itself," he wrote. "To cure these evils, we must first go to work on ourselves."

We no longer can pretend that public debates are conducted strictly on the merits, as if the only calculation politicians and pundits make is whether a policy is right or wrong. We have to note each and every time the public's ignorance and emotionalism are a factor in shaping political debates. If a politician takes a stand on an issue that is obviously calculated to play to the public's uninformed opinions, the media should point this out.

The People should be forced to face their own ignorance. Every time they are polled for their opinions they should be pressed to say what they actually know about the subject under discussion so we can know if they know what they are talking about. In the fall of 2007 a media poll found, for instance, that only 14 percent of Americans had confidence in Congress. But what did they know about what the Congress was doing? The poll didn't indicate. That was a serious shortcoming, considering that polls show most Americans usually do not even know which party controls Congress.

If the pollsters paid by the media fail to probe the public's ignorance, foundations should finance polls that do. If we are going to have a country that is run by polls we need polls that reveal what people don't know as well as what they think about things. If the media fail to publicize the polls that reveal the public's ignorance, foundations should help embarrass them into action by paying for full-page advertisements in the *New York Times* and other newspapers read by opinion makers to draw attention to the oversight.

Madison famously said that if men were angels, we wouldn't need government. It could as well be said that if politicians were angels we wouldn't have to worry about the voters' ignorance. Politicians would simply do the right thing. They wouldn't play on voters' fears or pander to their irrational biases. Unfortunately, angelic politicians are rare, so the issue that must absorb our energies is raising the level of ordinary voters to make them less ignorant.

Schooling by itself is not the answer. More than half of all Americans now have some college education. Yet they are no more knowledgeable about civics than Americans a half-century ago, when fewer than half of all citizens even graduated from high school (six in ten in 1940 never even got past the eighth grade). What's needed is specifically an emphasis on civics. Studies show that people who know civics are less easily manipulated by politicians.

Americans do not pick up civics lessons by osmosis. They have to be taught it. The time has arrived when we need to restore civics to school curricula. It is a major failing of the signal education reform of the Bush administration, No Child Left Behind, that civics was overlooked. The tests mandated under the law—tests that determine whether a school will receive federal funding—measure knowledge in only math and reading. Educators in consequence have emphasized those two subjects to the exclusion of others such as civics. This is unconscionable. But it is not the fault of the teachers. They are merely teaching to the test. Congress has to change the test. To paraphrase the old slogan of the supply-siders, if you want students to know more about civics, test for civics. If we test for civics we will communicate a powerful message that we as a society care about civics. Right now the message we are sending is that we don't.

Studies show that students who take civics courses in high school usually forget what they learn after a few years. This is an argument in favor of doing more civics, not less. Students should be required to take civics courses not only in high school but in college as well.

Most colleges have not placed an emphasis on civics (though some have and in recent years others have begun to do so). A beguiling but unproven assumption is that by the time students reach college they understand the basic facts about American government. This may once have been the case, when college was restricted to an elite group. But now that college is open to everybody we need to admit that many students arrive with an inadequate understanding of civics. Their ignorance of civics should no longer be regarded as somebody else's problem.

College students naturally would resist attending classes in civics. Few college teachers would want to teach the subject. But there is a way to teach civics without being boring or tedious. It is by requiring students to read newspapers and other news sources. We cannot of course force students to read anything. But if we test students on current events they will read what they have to in search of the answers. I recommend giving all freshmen in American colleges weekly current events tests. Those who pass with flying colors should be eligible for federal tuition subsidies paid for out of a special fund. Graduation should be made contingent on achieving at least a passing grade.

The federal law setting up the fund could be called the Too Many Stupid Voters Act. If this is too honest a title, I am confident the politicians could come up with something more popular. They're good at that. To draw broad support for the law the Congress could subsidize subscriptions to newspapers and public opinion journals. This would attract the support of large media corporations and non-profits. Newspaper reading has been in decline for a half-century. This law could help reverse the trend. Conservatives might object that the law would inadvertently benefit the so-called liberal media. To ease

their concerns a non-partisan commission could be set up
to design the tests. The commission could devise questions drawn from articles published by conservative pub-
lications like the *Weekly Standard* and *National Review* as
well as from the major newspapers and cable news shows.

Once students have graduated from college they should
be encouraged to form so-called democracy parties.
These are social gatherings at which issues are discussed
in depth. Studies show that voters who attend the parties
often change their minds about complicated subjects once
they have immersed themselves in information baths.

Benjamin Franklin said that in America we are all
politicians. That may have been true in the eighteenth
century. It is not true in the twenty-first. As John Dewey
predicted, consumers care little for politics and we are
all consumers now. The average American today spends
far more time thinking about what he shall buy than
about how he should vote. Most of us clip coupons. Few
of us clip the papers for news stories that might be worth
remembering later when we have to cast a ballot. While
we know the price of a gallon of milk, most of us don't
know basic civics facts. Could it be that the more we
identify as consumers the less we identify as voters? It
would seem so.

An aspect of a consumer culture is that we place a high
priority on entertainment. Whether Lindsey Lohan goes
to jail or not after being stopped for drunk driving cap-
tures the ordinary American's attention in a way politics

never does. It would be silly to berate voters for their inattentiveness (and unproductiveness as well) given that they are simply responding as human beings to a culture that places an emphasis on entertainment and consumption. But it is vital in designing a political system to take into account what is now obviously the citizen's natural political apathy.

What we know about voters is that they are primarily social rather than political creatures. Americans especially, despite a strong streak of individualism, are joiners, as Alexis de Tocqueville observed on his tour of the country in the 1830s. We aren't a civilization of hermits. We like to gather in groups. While some social scientists have recently become convinced that many of us now prefer "bowling alone," the metaphor used by Robert Putnam to describe people who resist joining groups, nearly all agree with Putnam that voluntary associations and churches "offer the best opportunities for civic skill building."

Americans formerly understood the connection between good citizenship and membership in political groups. That is why mass political parties were established in the 1820s and 1830s when suffrage was extended to millions of people. The parties did not neglect the entertainment aspects of politics, as we have seen. They turned elections into social events to attract the notice of voters and to sway them to their side. But the most important function of parties was giving voters a group with which they could identify politically. For a century and a half the arrangement, though imperfect, worked well. Voters voted in high percentages. They took a lively interest in politics. And most important of all they understood who was likely to advance their particular interests even when they did not follow closely the ins and outs of political debates. In short, they knew who buttered their bread.

As I have shown, the party system collapsed in the last half-century. As voters fled the party system they were given a pat on the head by many for exercising political independence from the bosses. If there is one clear lesson we should learn from our experience, however, it is that voters on their own know less and vote less.

Democrats fared worse under the new arrangement than Republicans, one of the multiple reasons for the Republican Party's ascendancy. Why was this? One reason stands out above all others: the decline of labor unions. Because Democrats had to a great extent relied on labor unions to organize voters and educate them about issues, the rapid collapse of the union movement in the 1970s and 1980s left the Democratic Party a hollowed-out shell of itself. At election time it increasingly found that it could call on the support of fewer and fewer union members. Thirty years ago 24 percent of the work force was enrolled in a union; today the number is 12 percent.

Can the parties be reconfigured? Republicans have shown the way. While the Democrats were losing the support that came from labor unions, Republicans were gaining the support of evangelical churches. Beginning in the 1980s these churches grew in membership and power, and as they did the Republican Party benefited immensely. (Some became so political that the IRS began to investigate their tax-free status.) Democrats now need to reinvigorate unions. They have to make it illegal to fire union organizers and make it easier for workers to join unions.

We *can* have a country of smart voters. I hope we make the changes needed to have this kind of country. It would be a nice place in which to live.

Epilogue

◆

On November 4, 2008, the American people elected Barack Hussein Obama the forty-fourth president of the United States of America. Immediately thereafter I started receiving emails from friends and strangers alike asking me if this didn't mean that the American people are actually pretty smart. I wish it were so. Nothing would make me happier than to reach this same self-satisfying conclusion. Alas, my own view is rather less encouraging. Indeed, I honestly cannot fathom how anybody who lived through the recent campaign could possibly find much evidence of a transformation in American voters' shallow approach to politics. Though the voters reached the same conclusion I did as to the best person for the job—a thing worthy of celebration, to be sure—I do not infer from this that they did so on the basis of a cool rationality or a knowledge of facts. It is a poor example of analytical rigor to judge the quality of the voters' thinking by the out-come of their collective decision. Were we to indulge in that bit of legerdemain we would quickly find ourselves in an intellectual cul-de-sac. For our purposes what is vital is how the voters reached their decision, not that they reached one with which we agree. To use myself as an illustration: Since I came of voting age in the 1970s I have cast a ballot in nine presidential elections. Five of those times I voted for the winner. But I do not delude myself that the public was smart five times and dumb the other times. It is entirely plausible that millions had dumb reasons for voting for my choice in some of those elections and intelligent reasons for voting against my choice in others. *Example:* I voted for Bill Clinton in 1992 because I thought he had a better grasp of the economic challenges facing the country than George H. W. Bush and I shared Clinton's core agenda, which I perceived to be basically liberal. I flatter myself in thinking that these were intelligent reasons for casting my vote as I did. But it is likely that millions voted for Clinton simply because they liked the saxophone-playing everyman better than the standoffish Bush, whom they blamed for the recession, fairly or not.

The trap from which we have to extricate ourselves is the beguiling belief that the electoral victory of our own choice signifies public intelligence. Unfortunately, this is an impulse almost impossible to resist. Not only is it natural to suppose that one's side in a contest is composed of all who are intelligent while the other side is made up of ignoramuses, but saying so is a ritual of American politics, accustoming us to think along these lines. A staple of our politics is the election-night victory party at which a smiling candidate, standing before an adoring crowd of supporters, announces to cheers that the voters have proved how smart they are. Should he lose in the next election these self-same voters will appear to have transmogrified into dumb voters—a metamorphosis that happens with remarkable speed and regularity, it would seem. But on the night of victory such is the cheery atmosphere that no one bothers to contest the candidate's extravagant claims. We can forgive the candidate in his moment of glory for thinking that his election is a sign of the voters' intelligence. But that is no excuse for the rest of us to adopt the same mindless habit of thinking.

This is not to say that there aren't smart choices and dumb choices. I am of the opinion that this year, of the two main candidates, the smart choice for president was Barack Obama. But proving why he was the better man is not something with which we are concerned here. Our focus is entirely on the way in which the public reached the decision to elect Obama president.

Placing the emphasis on *how* he was elected rather than on the fact that he was requires a degree of intellectual discipline. It requires us, for the moment, to set aside the aspect of this election outcome that is most palpable and easy to grasp—namely, the fact that the United States has just elected its first black president. This is necessary not because race is unimportant but because it is so important that we could easily slip into the habit of thinking about this election as if the only thing that mattered was Barack Obama's race.

Though Obama was careful not to allow himself to be regarded as the black candidate for president, his election as the first black president is nonetheless what is most striking. To those who remember watching television footage of Bull Connor's thugs letting loose German Shepherds on black protesters in Birmingham in 1963, the outcome of the election of 2008 is little short of miraculous. A person would have to be thick not to see the election of a black president as a remarkable turning point in our history. So great is the event that even Obama's opponent, John McCain, leaped to comment within hours of his defeat on the significance of Obama's election as a historic first in which we can all take pride.

Progress in overcoming racism is no small thing in a country founded on the racist belief that some are endowed by their creator with inferior gifts and that this inferiority marks them as naturally fit for slavery. Racism is, as many people have observed, America's original sin. But in my opinion so much has been made of racism as a corrosive element of American democracy that we have tended to underplay the significance of other flaws in our society that affect politics. One of the reasons I wrote this book is that it seemed to me—and still does—that we are so obsessed with race as a lens through which to see America that we subscribe to the unspoken conclusion that it is the only lens through which to view ourselves. Saying we have been obsessed with race may be too harsh. I do not mean to be harsh. I do not fault anyone for dwelling on racism in American society. Racism has decisively shaped our politics and may well have accounted for the lock the Republicans seemed to have on the presidency for many years. But the preoccupation with racism created an imbalance. Concerned with this imbalance, I deliberately downplayed racism as a factor in our politics in order to bring into the foreground political elements that are generally left hidden. Hence racism seldom surfaces in the multifaceted indictment of American politics made in the preceding pages of this book. In my five-part definition of stupidity (see pages 14-15), racism figures in just one, bone-headedness, "the susceptibility to meaningless phrases, stereotypes, irrational biases, and simplistic diagnoses and solutions that play on our hopes and fears."

All the while that we fixated on the problem of racism—a problem that was growing less severe over the past few decades—we all but ignored the public's ongoing indifference to civics—a problem that was growing more severe, as I have shown in this book. Both problems are measures of public ignorance. But one received constant attention in the media while the other received barely any at all. The pattern was replicated in schools. Curing us of racism became the passionate preoccupation of educators everywhere, leading to the adoption of multiculturalism as a fixed feature of school curriculums. At the same time, schools everywhere began dropping civics. Many groups formed to pressure schools to add African-American studies to the curriculum. None, as far as I know, demanded that civics be improved. It is almost comical to conjure up a scene of angry parents battering on the doors of administrators to Save Civics Now! The increase in black studies and the decrease in civics studies may well have been related to a certain extent. There being only so many hours in the school day, adding a class on black studies without cutting some other class was probably impossible. Choices had to be made. In many schools, undoubtedly, the choice made was to drop civics.

My chief criticism of the reaction to Obama's election is not that we have seized on it as a commentary on American race relations; that was to be expected and is altogether fitting. What troubles me is the instant note of triumphalism that accompanied it. Overnight we seem to have gone from a state of impurity to a state of grace. A country that can elect a Barack Obama is ipso facto a country of virtue, we tell ourselves. And as such, it may regard itself as the enlightened place it has always wanted to be. But when looking in the mirror these days what do we see? A preening peacock of a country: proud, self-congratulatory, and quite full of itself, if I may be permitted to put the matter so bluntly.

I do not write dispassionately about this development. I have had experience with it firsthand. As the campaign unfolded in the fall of 2008 I was distressed to see the public behaving in much the same way as it had in past campaigns, leading me to conclude that a sequel to this book might be warranted. When in early September it appeared that John McCain might well win the presidency I was encouraged to submit a new book proposal. A country that could elect McCain over Obama struck the liberals in publishing with whom I dealt as a country in need of criticism. But when Obama's prospects shifted following Wall Street's autumn meltdown, interest in my proposal ceased forthwith. I do not mean to personalize the issue. But it was eye-opening to see how quickly the mood of self-criticism turned to one of celebration, and this realization gave rise to a host of questions. Was the liberal critique of American politics so limited that the election of a single human being eased all of our concerns—or put us in such a frame of mind as to want to sidestep them? Had the audience for such a critique actually vanished, as publishers seemed to believe? Are liberals open to criticism of the nation only when elections result in the triumph of conservative candidates (as conservatives often aver)?

I share the elation of liberals in Obama's election. But shouldn't it be possible to feel hopeful without going gaga? Unfortunately, going gaga seems to have become the fashion of the day in many circles, including my own. Over Thanksgiving following the election I attended a wonderful dinner with about a dozen friends, all of whom confessed to feeling utter relief and excitement at the outcome of the presidential contest. Not even the daily barrage of gloomy economic news seemed to dim the halo that with suddenness seemed to appear in the firmament over our heads. Like Michelle Obama my friends finally felt proud of their country again. America had elected a liberal and obviously intelligent president who gives great speeches. And he's black! Whodathunkit?

We have, I believe, allowed ourselves to get carried away. The deluded and often grossly ignorant country that elected George W. Bush on the basis of misinformation and fear four short years before it elected Barack Obama did not up and disappear. Voters *en masse* did not suddenly start studying the globe to discover the location of countries we are bombing. They did not begin reading newspapers. They did not learn the names of their senators and congressman or the three branches of government. They did not turn to the Constitution to find out who declares war. They did not crack a history textbook to familiarize themselves with the key turning points of the last century or two. I presume that a majority still do not know that the only country that has used nuclear weapons in a war is their own.

Quibbling points all, since they got the main thing right—or so you may think if you are a liberal. But on what basis did the voters reach the conclusion that Obama was better for the country than McCain? If (many) political scientists are to be believed, it was primarily the lousy economy. If true, this in no way speaks to an improvement in the voters' civics skills. As noted earlier in this book, voters usually can be counted on to punish failure. One of the oldest patterns in American politics is the voters "throwing the bums out" when the economy turns sour.

That this election was about more than just the economy, no one would doubt. There were at least nine other factors shaping the outcome in Obama's favor: his uplifting speeches; his efficient campaign organization; his inspiring appeal to blacks, Hispanics, and the young; his ability to get his voters to the polls; his impressive equanimity; his ability to transcend race; his convincing performance at the presidential debates; his success in attracting donations; his themes of change and hope. Adding to this advantageous mix were all of McCain's obvious flaws: his lackluster speechmaking, the incoherence of his campaign, his selection of Sarah Palin, his bizarre decision to suspend his campaign, his endless freneticism, his mediocre debate performances, his disadvantage in campaign funds, his age. Finally, of course, there was the deep and sustained hostility to George W. Bush and the party that foisted him on the country.

But suppose for a moment that Wall Street had not come close to collapse. Would Obama still have won, despite his multitude of advantages and McCain's disadvantages? That it is not difficult to conceive of his having lost should give liberals pause. For it is not only conceivable that he might have lost—it is always conceivable to contrive the circumstances under which any candidate can lose—but *easy* to conceive of his having lost. That he won does not render as obsolete the critique that would have been made had he lost.

What elements might such a critique comprise? There are several of these, and I discuss them below. Interestingly, they suggest that, for all the obvious differences between the 2008 and past contests, the similarities were equally striking, if not more so. First, politics in 2008 was about emotions. Hillary Clinton won the New Hampshire primary by showing she had the capacity to cry. She won subsequent primaries in part simply by showing that she was a fighter seemingly unwilling ever to give up, even after it became mathematically impossible for her to secure her party's nomination. Voters appreciated her grit. Barack Obama started off in national politics four years earlier as a cerebral candidate known for giving wonkish speeches. According to biographer David Mendell, Obama even resisted using the slogan that became identified with him—"Yes we can"—because it sounded hokey.* But by the time he ran for president he had adopted an almost entirely emotional approach, at times sounding very much like the preachers he heard in black churches. He borrowed their cadences and rhythms to such a great extent it was difficult to remember at times that he was by training a law professor and not a preacher. Most of his speeches employed soaring rhetoric and glit-

---

*David Mendell, *Obama: From Promise to Power* (HarperCollins, 2007), p. 229.

tering generalities like "hope and change." During the primary season he appealed to the left-wing base of the Democratic Party by telling the crowd what they wanted to hear, harping particularly on their grievances with the Bush administration. He repeated over and over that he opposed George W. Bush's "dumb war" in Iraq and Bush's tax cuts for the wealthy. Everywhere he went he drew enormous crowds who seemed attracted as much by the spectacle as by anything else. What most people in attendance at his events seemed to crave was an emotional experience. Like evangelicals who place an emphasis on experience over doctrine, what counted was feelings. There is no evidence that Obama's supporters knew more about the issues or paid closer attention to campaign coverage than voters in general. A Zogby poll after the election found that a clear majority of Obama's supporters were unable even to say which party controlled the Congress. Like most voters in past elections they were far more likely to remember controversies that reflected badly on other candidates than those involving their own candidate. While an overwhelming majority of Obama's supporters knew about Sarah Palin's daughter's out-of-wedlock pregnancy, nearly three-fourths did not know that Vice President Joe Biden had been forced to drop out of his 1988 run for the White House after he was accused of plagiarism, though this fact was a critical bit of information for anyone making an assessment of Biden's fitness for high office (whereas the Palin daughter's behavior was irrelevant to her mother's qualifications). Though some critics griped about Zogby's methodology, his findings were entirely consistent with research results from past elections.

In the absence of substance, much of the campaign revolved around myths. Like nearly all successful candidates for the presidency Obama connected with audiences by exploiting the log cabin myth—"anybody can be president." Sometimes he was explicit, telling audiences that he was a child of poverty whose mother at one point had been forced to use food stamps. Usually, however, he took a more subtle approach, telling crowds the story of his unlikely emergence as a presidential candidate given the exotic contours of his background. By the end of the campaign nearly all Americans knew the story by heart: that his mother was from Kansas and his father from Kenya, and that he grew up in Hawaii and Indonesia. By framing his life story as an "anybody can be president" myth, Obama was able to turn his multicultural background, which might otherwise have been a disadvantage, into a powerful bond with audiences. One of the reasons he was able to defeat Hillary Clinton in the primaries is that he was able to put the log cabin myth to use and she wasn't. As the wife of a former president she couldn't convincingly pass herself off as an everywoman. What was she going to say? That she was a former first lady who had pulled herself up by her bootstraps? During the Pennsylvania primary she attempted to give voters the impression that she was just like them by knocking back a drink in a bar (in full view of the television cameras). The event drew wide attention, but she lacked the political dexterity of a George W. Bush to pull it off. She was more like his father, who unconvincingly feigned a love of pork rinds to convey the impression that he was a real down-to-earth American. The one way she could have tapped into the myth was by emphasizing the long odds she as a woman had to overcome to be taken seriously as a presidential contender. That's a story every American, man or woman, could have identified with. It was nearly as good as being born in a log cabin. To her misfortune, however, she could not afford to emphasize her gender without reinforcing the biggest doubt millions had about her—namely, that she was an ambitious vixen. In addition, such an approach would have gone against her deep convictions. As a feminist she had always been at pains to demonstrate that she was as good as a man, not that she was a woman deserving of special treatment by virtue of her gender.

The myth McCain told about himself was right out of a Hollywood script: the story of the self-sacrificing war hero. Like Obama, he used every opportunity to relate the key elements—in his case, how he had been shot down as a fighter pilot in Vietnam and then had endured unspeakable torture as a prisoner of war at the infamous Hanoi Hilton for five long unbearable years. There was no gainsaying his credibility as an authentic hero, but the facts about his naval career were more complicated than

McCain let on. Historian Mary Hershberger, one of the few scholars to undertake a close examination of McCain's wartime record, found strong evidence to substantiate a charge that McCain had been self-servingly selective in his narrative. Three examples follow. (1) *The Fire:* Three months before he became a POW in 1967, McCain was stationed on the aircraft carrier *USS Forrestal* when a fire broke out that led to the loss of 134 lives, one of the worst disasters in U.S. naval history. The fire began when some-one accidentally launched a rocket from a plane posi-tioned on the carrier deck. McCain in his memoirs related that the rocket hit his own plane, triggering (he claimed) the release of two bombs that turned the fire into a fatal conflagration. Actually, the rocket hit another plane, not McCain's. Why lie? Because McCain apparently did not want to admit that in the confused moments after the rocket took flight he must have accidentally triggered the release of the bomb from his own plane that caused mass destruction. (There was just one bomb; McCain mistak-enly referred to two.) (2) *The Aftermath:* After the deck caught fire McCain fled the scene, leaving the dangerous work of fighting the fire to others. A few days later, with-out leave, he caught a ride off the aircraft with a journal-ist for "some welcome R&R" in Saigon. McCain admits

---

*Mary Hershberger, "What Is the True Story of McCain's Wartime Experience?" History News Network (October 28, 2008), available on-line at http://hnn.us/roundup/entries/56255.html.

in his memoirs that he left the carrier but leaves the false impression that it was acceptable for him to do so. (3) *The POW Years:* Four days after his capture McCain was interviewed on camera by French journalist Francois Chalais. In his memoirs McCain described himself as combative with guards and says he declined to talk about the medical care he was receiving for his many wounds. During the campaign a clip from the interview turned up on YouTube. McCain, though obviously in pain, actually reported that he was receiving excellent care and good food.

Upon reading this you may wonder why you never heard of Hershberger or her debunking. The answer is that no one at either the main television stations or the major print media chose to give her a national platform. This is an indictment of the mainstream media. But it is also an indictment of the American public. Just as a people get the government they deserve, they also get the media they deserve. If the public wanted a media establishment willing to take on the myths politicians peddle, we would have such a media.

The biggest myth of campaign 2008, one of the granddaddy myths of all time, was the widespread belief that Barack Hussein Obama was a Muslim or that his religious identity was in question. Given the wall-to-wall coverage during the primaries of the controversial statements made by his pastor—his Christian pastor, *bien sûr!*—it is difficult to fathom the confusion that prevailed in many quarters about Obama's religion. And yet on the eve of the election, confusion reigned. Polls indicated that 7 percent of the voters in the key battleground states of Florida and Ohio and 23 percent in Texas believed that Obama was a Muslim. In addition, and worse, more than 40 percent in Florida and Ohio reported that they did not know what his religion was. The arithmetic is horrifying: 7 percent + 40 percent = a near majority guilty of gross ignorance.

Americans did not come by their confusion by accident. A deliberate campaign was launched by Republicans to convince people that Obama's faith was in question. But what are we to make of voters who could be so easily bamboozled? This was not after all a complicated issue. Obama was a Christian and he said so on numerous occasions. At the height of the controversy involving his pastor, Obama gave a speech in which he professed his deep faith in Christianity. Said speech was widely disseminated.

Distinctions are in order if we are to understand these categories of uninformed voters. One such group, mercifully small, consisted of voters who were so busy living their lives in isolation from politics that when they were asked what Obama's religion was and they answered that they did not know it was because they really did not know, having paid little attention to the 2008 campaign. A second group, a little larger, was composed of voters who were either so racist or so suspicious of outsiders that they were prepared to believe almost anything about him. When they heard that Obama—a politician about whom they knew little, given his recent introduction as a national figure—shared the faith of the terrorists who attacked us on 9/11, they instantly believed it because it sounded negative, blocking out all contrary evidence. The third group, by far the largest, was made up of people who didn't know what to think, having heard conflicting information about Obama's religion. As one addled fellow told a *Washington Post* reporter, "It's like you're hearing about two different men with nothing in common. It makes it impossible to figure out what's true, or what you can believe."

One is grateful that the third group was the largest. It gives one hope that for the vast majority of Americans information remains a vital consideration in the formation of opinion. But we are back again to the blasted problem that misinformation is as apt to be swallowed by people as factual information. More troubling, voters don't seem to know where to turn for reliable information. Why, we should all be asking, didn't people who were confused about Obama's religious affiliation know enough to consult a good reliable newspaper like the *Washington Post* or the *New York Times* to find out what professional journalists had reported? Has suspiciousness of the media gone so far that voters think they cannot trust mainstream journalists to give them the basic facts about a presidential candidate's religion? If so, then we are in far more trouble than anyone has imagined. This isn't Nazi Germany or the Soviet Union. The media can be trusted to get basic facts right most of the time. If people think journalists cannot be trusted to do this, then they are out of touch with reality.

An indication of the low level of public debate in this campaign was the plethora of trivial issues that time and again took center stage, providing fresh evidence for one of the key points I make in the book: that the issues most susceptible to public debate are those which require little or no knowledge. Rather than discuss in detail Obama's tax proposals or McCain's health plan (yes, he had one), we found ourselves preoccupied with such weighty concerns as whether Hillary's tearing up in New Hampshire was real or contrived, whether Obama was a genuine American considering that he couldn't bowl, and the meaning of the Obamas' fist bump. Pundits on television spent days dwelling on each of these subjects. Then came Sarah Palin's selection. Palin instantly became a magnet for shallow stories, to a degree unprecedented in modern American history. People commented on her hair, her kids, her husband, and her speaking style. When it was revealed late in the campaign that this self-described hockey-mom had been outfitted in fancy clothes purchased at expensive stores ($75,062 expended at Neiman Marcus alone, by one report), pundits snarled and snorted like happy pigs in a mud bath. Voters seemed drawn to watch.

Palin was a phenom! What made her such? Her personality and her story, of course. In September the *New York Times* sent reporters out around the country to find out what voters made of Palin. Tana Krueger, a Wisconsin mother of six who had liked Hillary Clinton in the primaries, said that she was ready to give Palin her vote. Why? Because "she's me. I can just really relate to everything in her life, children with disabilities, teenage pregnancy." It apparently did not occur to Ms. Kruger to consider more substantive factors in selecting a president such as (a) experience, (b) agenda, or (c) ability, to name just a few.

Love her or hate her, no one was neutral about Palin. At the height of the financial crisis in October, what everybody was looking forward to was her debate with Biden. It is worthwhile pausing for a moment to review what happened.

Expectations were high that the debate would make great entertainment. What might either Biden or Palin say or do? Biden was famous for saying whatever came into his head. And as for Palin: Who knew which Palin was going to show up? Would it be the Palin who so impressed Republicans at the GOP convention that she instantly became a celebrity politician, the Republican Party's Barack Obama? Or would it be the Palin who appeared almost dazed during the Katie Couric interview on CBS? Some 70 million Americans tuned in to find out—the largest audience ever for a veep debate and the second-largest audience ever for a political debate of any kind. (The debate drawing the largest audience was the 1980 face-off between Ronald Reagan and Jimmy Carter, when 80 million watched.) Everybody knew who was the chief draw. It was Palin. People were fascinated with her.

Who was she? Did she know what she was talking about? Would she take charge or falter under the klieg lights? Most important of all was this simple question: Would she fall flat on her ass?

It took exactly ten seconds to find out. "Hey, can I call you Joe?" she asked Biden as she took her place. It was pitch-perfect. Confident and folksy Palin had showed up. Yes, we'd have a real humdinger of a debate. Or at least a good show.

Biden, natch, was more substantive. He'd been in Congress since he was 29, after all. How could he not know the details of public policy by now? He'd have to have been a dolt not to be able to answer moderator Gwen Ifill's questions. But since when were debates about substance? They were mostly about style, and Biden's style on this night was mainly (though not wholly; the man just couldn't entirely restrain himself) boring. Being boring was the goal. The last thing Biden wanted to do was make news. Making news would mean he'd bloviated again. So he kept his answers blessedly brief and avoided, for the most part, saying anything that could be used against him or Obama later. His opening was especially dull as he recited the . . . four . . . basic . . . criteria . . . his running mate had laid down for the bailout package. Fortunately, he didn't lose his way and remembered each of the points he wanted to make, though viewers weren't sure he would until he got through them all. (Democrats in the audience sighed with relief.) Later, he showed a little passion in denouncing the Iraq War and McCain's healthcare plan.

And Palin? She was folksy—boy, was she folksy! It was Ma and Pa Kettle politics from here to Sunday, don't you know. She didn't actually use the word "betcha," though some people thought she had. But she did say "I'll bet you," "darn right," "Main Streeters like me," "bless their hearts," and "doggone it." No one who talked like that had appeared on network TV since *Hee Haw* went off the air. The difference between Biden and Palin in the end was this. He spoke about middle-class Americans in Scranton and other places he'd visited. She sounded like she was a middle-class American. She talked like Joe Six Pack in such a way that when she literally referred to "Joe Six Pack" she didn't sound condescending as most politicians do when they used the shorthand moniker. Indeed, she didn't seem to sound like any other politician at all most of the time. Yet the fascinating thing was that she actually borrowed heavily from the standard politician's bag of rhetorical tricks, which was obvious to those willing to get past her personality—but there was fat chance of that!

Item: When she didn't want to answer a question she changed the subject:

> *Ifill:* Governor, please if you want to respond to what he said about Senator McCain's comments about healthcare?

Palin: I would like to respond about the tax increases.

For the record: Biden hadn't mentioned tax increases.

Item: Anticipating that she might be called out on her evasiveness, she made evasiveness seem revolutionary, almost historic: "I may not answer the questions that either the moderator or you want to hear, but I'm going to talk straight to the American people and let them know my track record." Hoorah!

Item: When Biden went after McCain for supporting the Iraq War, she accused him of flip-flopping: "Because here you voted for the war and now you oppose the war. You're one who says, as so many politicians do, I was for it before I was against it or vice-versa. Americans are craving that straight talk and just want to know, hey, if you voted for it, tell us why you voted for it and it was a war resolution."

Item: When Biden argued that McCain would continue the war and tax policies of the Bush administration, she pulled out a classic sound bite obviously prepared in advance to put Biden on the defensive: "Say it ain't so, Joe, there you go again pointing backwards again. You prefer-enced your whole comment with the Bush administration. Now doggone it, let's look ahead and tell Americans what we have to plan to do for them in the future." Could Reagan have said it any better?

Item: She played the outsider card repeatedly: "I do respect your years in the U.S. Senate, but I think Americans are craving something new and different," and later, "Oh, yeah, it's so obvious I'm a Washington outsider."

Item: Like Spiro Agnew and a hundred Republican imitators down through the years, she declared war on the media: "I like being able to answer these tough questions without the filter, even, of the mainstream media kind of telling viewers what they've just heard. I'd rather be able to just speak to the American people like we just did."

Item: When Gwen Ifill asked the candidates if they'd ever had a reason to change their minds about something, Biden gave a thoughtful and honest answer, saying he'd come to realize that judicial candidates should be asked where they stand on specific issues; they shouldn't be confirmed simply because they were people in good standing. And Palin? She started off in a way that made you think she was about to be honest, but it was just a feint to throw you off guard as she took refuge behind a meaningless string of nouns, verbs, and adjectives piled on high like whipped cream covering an ugly cake: "There have been times where, as mayor and governor, we have passed budgets that I did not veto and that I think could be considered as something that I quasi-caved in, if you will, but knowing that it was the right thing to do in order to progress the agenda for that year and to work with the legislative body, that body that actually holds the purse strings. So there were times when I wanted to zero-base budget, and to cut taxes even more, and I didn't have enough support in order to accomplish that." Whaaat?

The post-debate yakkers on TV said afterward that Biden had done better on substance than Palin and the audience in instant polls gave Biden the night, declaring him the clear winner. CBS reported that 46 percent of uncommitted voters believed Biden won; only 21 percent thought Palin had. A CNN poll of all voters judged Biden the victor by a stunning margin of 51 to 36 percent.

But the voters liked Palin's personality more. The same CNN poll that had Biden winning by a clear majority indicated that 54 percent found Palin more likeable. Only 36 percent found Biden more likeable. It was the old Bush-Kerry pattern once again. In 2004 John Kerry clearly had cleaned George W. Bush's clock at their debates. Everybody knew Kerry had won. But people liked Bush better. And now they liked Palin better. Did it really matter who won?

It seemed to. By the end of the campaign the media consensus was that Palin was a drag on the ticket. Voters, however much they liked Palin, concluded she wasn't ready for prime time. But the public's ultimate judgment demonstrated the ordinary voters' weaknesses as well as their strengths. Voters showed wisdom in deciding that Palin wasn't presidential material (though 65 percent of Republicans persisted in believing she was ready to be president). On the other hand, they turned against her only because they didn't like the Palin they saw in her interviews with hard-news journalists like Katie Couric and Charles Gibson, when she repeatedly stumbled her way through her answers like a kid at school taking a test she was unprepared for. In short, voters relied on the superficial impressions gained through television to guide their decisions. Presumably, had Palin been able to answer the questions more convincingly, voters would have made the judgment that she was ready to be president even though her experience in national and international affairs was wholly deficient. For the country's sake, we should be grateful that Palin's deficiencies were obvious to the television viewer. But suppose they weren't? Suppose like George W. Bush she was a bit more talented as a bullshitter. She might easily have passed muster then. This scares the daylights out of me. Had the elderly McCain been elected, Palin would have been a heartbeat away from the presidency.

Those who think I have exaggerated the case I am making may choose to believe what they wish. But evidence abounds that my view of the 2008 electorate closely approximates the views of those running the Obama and McCain campaigns. And they presumably were expert in analyzing the electorate. I do not mean that they openly made statements like those I have made here. They were careful never to do so, though Rick Davis, McCain's campaign manager, was quoted as saying that the election was fundamentally about personality, not issues. But we can glean their assumptions about the electorate's capacity easily enough by studying the means they used to shape public opinion.

I will not have to do much to persuade liberals that Mc-Cain's campaign took a dim view of the voter. I probably do not even have to persuade conservatives of this. What, after all, did McCain's argument in favor of his candidacy amount to? That Obama was an unknown man who palled around with terrorists. That Obama was a wild-eyed radical. That Obama was green but Palin wasn't. These arguments, which together may be said to have constituted the McCain campaign corpus, were evidently geared to appeal to low-information voters. The explicit resort to fear, which triggers impulses in the brain that override reasoning faculties, was especially revealing. They reflected the campaign's desperation as events increasingly favored the Democratic Party's prospects. (California Republican Party advertisement: "The only difference between Obama and Osama is BS.")

In the spring of 2008 Emory University's Drew Westen had predicted that the Republicans would resort to fear in the general election because they had nothing else to run on. They couldn't brag about the economy or Iraq or Afghanistan. He flat-out predicted that the election would therefore be one of the dirtiest in American history. It was. By October, McCain's campaign had so riled up people about Obama that its rallies had turned ugly, with some supporters making threats against Obama's life. At one point McCain himself felt compelled to grab the microphone from a woman badmouthing Obama at a town hall meeting. Obama, he reassured her, was a decent family man whom Americans could respect should he win the White House. From the crowd came boos.

But what about Obama? Unlike McCain he did not appeal to peoples' fears. He gave several speeches of a high quality, including the one on race that was the equal of any given by a presidential candidate in American history and easily was clearer and more honest than any speech about race ever delivered by a president of the United States. But most of his speeches were light on policy details, and many consisted of little more than feel-good slogans: "Yes, we can." "Change we can believe in." "Change we need."

I do not fault Obama for trying to be as general as possible in his speeches. All politicians try to avoid making detailed policy promises that can come back to haunt them later. But as the anti-politician politician, Obama claimed to be different from other pols. In fact, he often played the game exactly as others do. Why didn't he worry that he would be accused of being an ordinary politician? Because he had supreme confidence in his own ability to convince voters that he was different. Voters wouldn't notice that he was actually vague about his plans as long as they were excited about his general message of hope.

Hope and change hope and change hope and change hope and change hope and change hope and change— repeated over and over in speeches and in advertisements— formed the virtual repertoire of the entire Obama campaign.

Whatever the issue, the terrible wars in Iraq and Afghanistan, Guantanamo, Abu Ghraib, the failing economy, you name it, hope and change (hope and change. *n. singular*) was always the answer. It was a simple enough message to qualify as the lyrics of a hit pop tune. What did Obama mean to do about any of these problems? That was always left vague enough for people to draw their own conclusions. And Obama knew the voters would be content with vagueness. Our voters, following a period of sturm and drang, demand nothing more than to be soothed as they were after Watergate by Jimmy Carter's beguiling and reassuring smile. Like Carter, Obama possesses a dazzling smile that he has used knowingly to great effect.

Did he mean to end the war in Iraq? He did. In sixteen months. Which sounded precise and won the acclaim of the anti-war crowd. But was his policy any different from Hillary Clinton's? Was it really any different from George W. Bush's? One presumed that at least the latter was true, but then when Obama was elected one of his first decisions was to retain Bush's secretary of war. How different in actuality, then, was Obama's war policy from Bush's by 2008?

One wishes not to so generalize Barack Obama's profile as to make him indistinguishable from other pols. He clearly is different, and not only because when he looks in the mirror the face staring back at him is black. But he behaved just like an ordinary pol on so many occasions that one begins to suspect that his chief calculations were more similar to theirs than different. When the McCain campaign began saying hateful things about him, for example, he responded with the pedestrian comment that the American people were smarter than to fall for lies.

Did he really believe the American people are smart? Of course not. Like McCain, he counted on people not being smart.

Through the spring and summer Obama had presented himself as a victim of Republican lies. But as the fall campaign wore on and Democrats began to worry about his electability (many recalling Hillary Clinton's warnings in the spring that he was a weak candidate), his campaign began playing with the truth more and more—and getting caught by the same media watchdogs who had earlier gone after McCain relentlessly. The week following a *New York Times* exposé singling McCain out for using Karl Rove–style tactics, Obama was roasted for his adoption of those same tactics. Running on Spanish-language TV was an Obama commercial citing two grossly anti-immigrant statements by Rush Limbaugh that were flashed on the screen:

" . . . Mexicans stupid and unqualified."—Rush Limbaugh
"Shut up, or get out!"—Rush Limbaugh

As the Annenberg Public Policy Center of the University of Pennsylvania's FactCheck.org website explained, both quotes had been taken out of context. Limbaugh hadn't been serious. He'd made the statements in the course of satirizing the arguments made by others. Worse than being caught out by one of the watchdogs the campaign had been citing to prove it was a victim of dastardly politics was that Limbaugh had been able to crow in the pages of the *Wall Street Journal* that he'd been misquoted. That was like being taken to the woodshed by your worst enemy. Even liberals had to admit ("grrrrr") that Limbaugh had been wronged, though they also argued, with justification, that he'd gone too far when he'd claimed that Obama had been trafficking in hate comparable to the segregationists of the 1950s. That was ridiculous. But since when was it acceptable for Barack Obama, candidate of hope and change, to be caught playing the same kind of politics as Rush Limbaugh?

If that were the only example of Obama mangling the facts, no one could have accused him of gutter politics. But he was also lambasted for misstating McCain's position on Social Security in a speech before the elderly in Florida. McCain wanted to allow young people to invest a portion of their Social Security taxes in the stock market. Given the bad week the market had just gone through, that idea now sounded harebrained. But Obama charged that "if my opponent had his way," the elderly currently on Social Security would be in a vulnerable position and begging their families for support. As the Annenberg website noted, "That's not true. The plan proposed by President Bush and supported by McCain in 2005 would not have allowed anyone born before 1950 to invest any part of their Social Security taxes in private accounts. All current retirees would be covered by the same benefits they are now."

Obama probably knew that his campaign was making false statements about Limbaugh. He certainly knew that he himself was misconstruing McCain's record. But he also knew that he could probably get away with these and other misstatements because few voters would ever become aware of the errors unless a pattern developed sufficient to create a new media narrative. A candidate for president does not have to be pure. He need only be pure enough to pass muster with a generally incurious public.

My goal in writing this book was the rather immodest one of helping to stoke a national conversation about the limits of public opinion. In this I have had some small measure of success. Judging by their columns, several of the leading op-ed writers in the country read the book. And it's possible, though I've been unable to confirm it, that even the writers of the hit TV show *Boston Legal* did so. In one of the series' last episodes Alan Shore (James Spader) delivers a rousing speech to a jury that reflects many of the same arguments I used and cites several of the same statistics. Many teachers are using the book in their classes, I have been told.

My task was made easier with George W. Bush in the White House. Many wanted to know how such a thing as his election to the highest office in the land had come to pass. Now that we have Obama in the White House there is naturally less interest in the subject. This is a shame. From where I sit, the errors to which the public is prone—errors rooted in a profound indifference to the rational discussion of politics—remain every bit as alarming today as they were a year ago or five years ago. Our problems are not getting simpler. If anything, they are getting harder. Only a public that is able to follow a complicated narrative will be able to meaningfully take part in a robust debate about the solutions.

Acknowledgments

◆

None of the people I am about to name are responsible for my saying the things I say in this book. If you want to throw brickbats, toss them my way. But each in their own way helped me write a better book. I am grateful to all of them.

A casual conversation with Lara Heimert at a history convention led to the writing of the book. A subsequent conversation on the phone gave me the focus I needed to carry off the project. It was one of only a few conversations I have ever had in which a lightbulb went off in my head as in a cartoon, suddenly flooding my mind with ideas. I was particularly pleased to find myself working with Lara because I had had her father as a teacher. Alan Heimert was one of the giants of the profession.

Three of my friends kindly agreed to review the manuscript: Bernard Weisberger, Gil Troy, and Leonard Steinhorn. I was honored to have their help and am astounded by their generosity. All three lead busy lives. Finding time to read and critique this book cannot have been easy. This is the fourth time I have asked Bernie to review a manuscript. He is a mensch for saying yes every time. An email exchange with another friend, Clyde Griffen, helped convince me that a central problem we face is that voters are now left largely on their own, a point I found myself coming back to time and again as I wrote the book.

Liz Stein edited the manuscript under a tight deadline. I have never been more pleased with an editor's work. It was easy to revise the manuscript after she had gotten through with it.

Christine Arden copyedited the manuscript. Going through her notes was an education in grammar and vocabulary.

This is the first book I have done with William Clark, my agent. I thank him for his help and I thank Ed Victor, my previous agent, for referring me to William.

I also want to thank my high school history teacher, Milo Okkema. He introduced me to the work of Walter Lippmann and was the first to get me thinking about public opinion, a subject to which he devoted endless classroom hours—to his students' great benefit. I also want to mention my debt to the late Thomas A. Bailey, who got me excited years ago about the role myths play in our culture and in the formation of public opinion. I wish he were around to read this book.

Mark Carnes deserves a mention, too. It was Mark's invitation several years ago to contribute a chapter to *The Columbia History of Post–World War II America* that plunged me into research about the impact of television on our politics.

Finally, I want to thank my husband John. Eight years and still going strong! It has helped immensely to come home each night to intelligent (and lively!) discussions about politics. But it is his support, of course, that I want to honor. He's a terrific partner.

Sources

◆

Because this book is intended for the general public I have not included detailed academic footnotes. But I want to draw the attention of the reader to the key sources I consulted. In most cases the statistics and quotes I cite in the book can easily be located in a matter of seconds through a Google search.

CHAPTER 1: THE PROBLEM

The surveys documenting the public's ignorance about Saddam and 9/11 were done under the auspices of the Program on International Policy Attitudes (PIPA), a joint program of the Center for International and Security Studies at [the University of] Maryland (CISSM) and the Center on Policy Attitudes (COPA). The polls were carried out by Knowledge Networks, a market research firm based in Menlo Park, California. The discussion of Walter Lippmann and John Dewey is drawn from Brett Gary's *The Nervous Liberals: Propaganda Anxieties from World War I to the Cold War* (Columbia University Press, 1999), pp. 243–250, as well as from Lippmann's *Public Opinion* (1955; rpt. Macmillan, 1947) and *The*

Public Philosophy (1955; rpt. Mentor, 1972). Lippmann's suspicions of the masses were echoed in Fritz Lang's movie *Dr. Mabuse: The Gambler* (1922), in which a wily doctor hypnotizes an entire theater audience. (The film is placed in historical context in Peter Buchka's 1998 documentary, *The Haunted Screen: German Film After World War I.*) A good general introduction to the role of propaganda in modern societies is Mark Wollaeger's *Modernism, Media and Propaganda* (Princeton University Press, 2006). See in particular his discussion of the French philosopher Jacques Ellul, who observed: "Developments [in the modern world] are not merely beyond man's intellectual scope; they are also beyond him in volume and intensity; he simply cannot grasp the world's economic and political problems. Faced with such matters, he feels his weakness, his inconsistency, his lack of effectiveness. He realizes that he depends on decisions over which he has no control, and that realization drives him to despair. Man cannot stay in this situation too long. He needs an ideological veil to cover harsh reality, some consolation, a *raison d'être*, a sense of values. And only propaganda offers him a remedy for a basically intolerable situation" (p. 12).

The book in which I made the comment about Santa Claus is *"I Love Paul Revere, Whether He Rode or Not"* (HarperCollins, 1991), p. 199. A good introduction to the study of myths in American history is James Oliver Robertson's *American Myth, American Reality* (Hill and Wang, 1980). Thomas Bailey's *The Man in the Street* (Macmillan, 1948) shows how myths have long affected our foreign policy. Bailey sums up his views in his presidential address to the Organization of American Historians, "The Mythmakers of American History," *Journal of American History* (June 1968), pp. 5–21. On the question of the public's appetite for truth, see *Arthur Miller's Adaptation of An Enemy of the People by Henrik Ibsen* (Penguin Books, 1950).

CHAPTER 2: GROSS IGNORANCE

Barbara Tuchman discusses wooden-headedness in *The March of Folly: From Troy to Vietnam* (Knopf, 1984), pp. 7–8. The best single guide to the surveys measuring public ignorance is *What Americans Know About Politics and Why It Matters* (Yale University Press, 1996) by Michael X. Delli Carpini and Scott Keeter. The public's ignorance about the length of congressional terms is cited on p. 71; its unfamiliarity with Gorbachev's name, on p. 62, with O'Connor, on p. 78, with Rehnquist, on p. 93, and with Powell and Cheney, on p. 79. The authors' summaries of their findings (that only 5 percent, for instance, could answer three-fourths of the questions about economics) are reported on pp. 71, 79, 82, and 85. How Americans rank presidents is cited here: www.polling report.com/wh-hstry.htm. The low reading levels of Americans are reported in a study by the National Endowment for the Arts: "Reading At Risk: A Survey of Literary Reading in America" (June 2004). The dismaying statistics about the young are cited by David T.Z. Mindich in *Tuned Out: Why Americans Under 40 Don't Follow the News* (Oxford University Press, 2005), *passim*. The indifference of most Americans to newspapers is laid out in "The State of the News Media, 2004" (www.stateofthenewsmedia.org/narrative_newspapers_audience.asp?cat=3&media=2). Low turnout among youth in elections is reported at the website of The Center for Information & Research on Civic Learning & Engagement in a report: "The Youth Vote 2004" (www.stateofthenewsmedia.org/narrative_newspapers_audience.asp?cat=3&media=2). The unfamiliarity with McCain-Feingold is cited by Mindich on p. 18 of *Tuned Out*. The Pew study of Internet use, "For Many Home Broadband Users, the Internet Is a Primary News Source," may be found here: www.pewinternet.org/pdfs/PIP_News.and.Broad band.pdf. Thomas Patterson's research findings are summarized in *The Vanishing Voter* (Knopf, 2002), pp. 24–25.

Two books are vital to understanding the actual condition of Social Security: Max Skidmore's *Social Security and Its Enemies: The Case for America's Most Efficient Insurance Program* (Westview Press, 1999) and Dean Baker and Mark Weisbrot's *Social Security: The Phony Crisis* (University of Chicago Press, 2001). Baker and Weisbrot, in disagreement with me, argue that the Trust Fund is not actually a fiction because the money loaned from the Fund to the U.S. Treasury is backed by IOUs. In their view, that makes the IOUs no different than U.S. Treasury bonds.

CHAPTER 3: ARE THE VOTERS IRRATIONAL?

V. O. Key Jr. in *The Responsible Electorate* (Belknap, 1966) and Samuel Popkin in *The Reasoning Voter* (University of Chicago Press, 1994) make the argument that the voters are rational. Popkin tells the story about Reagan and the microphone on p. 168. Key reports on the farmers' vote switching in 1940 on p. 45. Popkin explains heuristics in Chapter 4 and lists the mistakes voters make on pp. 91–94. One of the earliest studies of voter rationality is *The American Voter* by Angus Campbell, Philip E. Converse, Warren E. Miller, and Donald E. Stokes (John Wiley & Sons, 1964). The book summarizes the findings of the University of Michigan's Survey Research Center. On pp. 252–253 the authors discuss the limits of public understanding, and on p. 288 they suggest why elections are usually a referendum on the party in power. The poll about the fictitious Public Affairs Act of 1975 is discussed by Alan Wolfe in *Does American Democracy Still Work?* (Yale University Press, 2006). Bryan Caplan discusses the voters' ignorance of economics in *The Myth of the Rational Voter: Why Democracies Choose Bad Policies* (Princeton University Press, 2007).

CHAPTER 4: THE IMPORTANCE OF MYTHS

In addition to the books about myths cited earlier, see Dixon Wecter's *The Hero in America: A Chronicle of Hero-Worship* (Charles Scribner's and Sons, 1972), which shows the importance in American culture of stories, tall tales, and myths. A good introduction to the change that took place in American politics once the masses took power is John William Ward's *Andrew Jackson: Symbol for an Age* (Oxford University Press, 1953). Ted Widmer offers a lively account of the log cabin campaign of 1840 in *Martin Van Buren* (Times Books, 2005), pp. 131–140. The profile of Iowa Governor Vilsack in the *New York Times* appeared on June 24, 2004. Howard Dean's reference to himself as a rural person was cited by David Brooks in the *New York Times* on December 9, 2003. Edward Pessen reports on the wealth of presidents in *The Log Cabin Myth: The Social Backgrounds of the Presidents* (Yale University Press, 1986). The writer John Keats offers an acerbic picture of American classes in *The Insolent Chariots* (Lippincott, 1958). Paul Krugman discusses the Great Compression in his book *The Conscience of a Liberal* (W. W. Norton, 2007), pp. 37–53. According to the Federal Reserve Bank's 2006 Survey of Consumer Finances, 715 families own 70 percent of bonds and 51 percent of stocks (*Wall Street Journal*, April 5, 2006). Joseph Ellis describes Madison's theories in *American Creation: Triumphs and Tragedies at the Founding of the Republic* (Knopf, 2007), *passim*. Eugene McCarthy's speech is quoted here: news.minnesota.publicradio.org/features/2005/06/15_ol sond_genemccarthy. Lyndon Johnson's speech is quoted here: www.lbjlib.utexas.edu/johnson/archives.hom/speeches.hom/ 680331.asp.

CHAPTER 5: GIVING CONTROL TO THE PEOPLE

On the impact of polls on American politics, see Lizabeth Cohen, *A Consumers' Republic* (Knopf, 2003), pp. 341–344. The *Wall Street Journal/NBC Nightly News Poll* was published on April 26, 2006, in the same broadcast on which oil analyst Phil Flynn was interviewed: www.msnbc.msn.com/id/12502356/. The Reuters story appeared on April 27, 2006: www.nytimes.com/reuters/washington/politics-energy-congress.html. Thomas Friedman's column appeared in the *New York Times* on May 3, 2006. Rush Limbaugh was quoted in a front-page *New York Times* story on May 5, 2006. Cheney's claim that the American people have spoken appeared in the *New York Times* on March 14, 2006. The gap between what politicians say and what they do is noted in Alan Wolfe's *Does American Democracy Still Work?* (Yale University Press, 2006), p. 65. The effect of primaries on politics is discussed by Joe Klein in *Politics Lost* (Doubleday, 2006), p. 31. The proliferation of primaries is documented in Lyn Ragsdale's *Vital Statistics on the Presidency* (Congressional Quarterly, 1998), p. 40. The *New York Times* poll of Iowa voters was published on the front page on November 14, 2007.

CHAPTER 6: THE POWER OF TELEVISION

For background on the story told in this chapter, see Rick Shenkman, "Television, Democracy and Presidential Politics," in *The Columbia History of Post–World War II America*, ed. Mark Carnes (Columbia University Press, 2007), where citations are provided for both the primary and secondary sources quoted in this chapter. The studies by Kurt and Gladys Lang are reprinted in their book *Television and Politics* (Transaction Publishers, 2002). Mary Ann Watson tells the story of the Kennedy/Nixon debate in *The Expanding Vista: American Television in the Kennedy Years* (Oxford University Press, 1990). Edwin Diamond and Stephen Bates chronicle the history of the television spot in *The Spot: The Rise of Political Advertising on Television* (MIT Press, 1984). Kathleen Hall Jamieson's landmark study, *Packaging the Presidency: A History and Criticism of Presidential Campaign Advertising* (Oxford University Press, 1996), provides the details about the ads run against Dukakis. Criticism of the effects of television on American politics and society can be found in Neil Postman's *Amusing Ourselves to Death: Public Discourse in the Age of Show Business* (Viking, 1985).

CHAPTER 7: OUR DUMB POLITICS: THE BIG PICTURE

The study showing a decline in the reading level of presidential speeches, "Presidential Debates Rank at Grade School Level," can be found here: www.yourdictionary.com/about/news011.html. Bill Clinton's comedy routine was noted by the *Washington Post* on March 23, 1998 (www.washingtonpost.com/wp-srv/politics/special/clinton/stories/gridiron032398.htm). Reagan's comment about acting is cited by Richard Reeves in *President Reagan: The Triumph of Imagination* (Simon and Schuster, 2005), p. 218. Reagan's presidential debates are chronicled by Alan Schroeder in *Presidential Debates* (Columbia University Press, 2000). Rush Limbaugh's audience is analyzed in "Call-In Political Talk Radio: Background, Content, Audiences, Portrayal in Mainstream Media" (www.annenbergpublicpolicycenter.org/03_political_communication/archive/1996_03_political-talk-radio_rpt.PDF). The CBS interview with the driver who refused to give up her car was broadcast on May 4, 2006 (www.cbsnews.com/stories/2006/05/04/eveningnews/main1589618.shtml).

CHAPTER 8: OUR MINDLESS DEBATE ABOUT 9/11

The Scripps-Howard poll is cited in an article in *Time*, "Why the 9/11 Conspiracies Won't Go Away," September 3, 2006 (www.time.com/time/magazine/article/0,9171,1531304,00.html). German public opinion concerning 9/11 is cited by Reuters, July 23, 2003 (www.boston.com/news/daily/23/911poll.htm). The 2005 Gallup Poll about the attitudes of Muslims is cited in the *New York Times*, June 8, 2006. Walter Laqueur lays out his case in *No End to War: Terrorism in the Twenty-First Century* (Continuum, 2003), pp. 25–28. Bernard Lewis's views are laid out in *What Went Wrong? Western Impact and Middle Eastern Response* (Oxford University Press, 2002). Thomas Friedman's views on terrorism, familiar to readers of his *New York Times* column, are collected in *Longitudes and Attitudes: Exploring the World After September 11* (Farrar, Straus and Giroux, 2002). Ivan Eland's case is made in *The Empire Has No Clothes: U.S. Foreign Policy Exposed* (Independent Institute, 2004). The quotation from Stephen Kinzer is from an interview he gave to the History News Network on September 26, 2005 (hnn.us/articles/15825.html). He explains his views at length in two enlightening books: *All the Shah's Men* (John Wiley & Sons, 2003) and *Overthrow: America's Century of Regime Change from Hawaii to Iraq* (Times Books, 2007). Marc Sageman summarizes his research in a statement to the National Commission on Terrorist Attacks Upon the United States, July 9, 2003 (www.global security.org/security/library/congress/9-11_commission/030709-sageman.htm).

CHAPTER 9:
WE CAN'T EVEN TALK ABOUT HOW STUPID WE ARE

Thomas Friedman's column, "Dubai and Dunces," appeared in the *New York Times* on March 15, 2006 (www.uaecommunity

.blogspot.com/2006/03/dubai-and-dunces.html). The celebration of democracy is noted throughout Fareed Zakaria's *The Future of Freedom* (W. W. Norton, 2003). Gil Troy discusses the Founding Fathers' views on virtue in *See How They Ran: The Changing Role of the Presidential Candidate* (Harvard University Press, 1996), pp. 8–20. See also Rick Shenkman, *"I Love Paul Revere, Whether He Rode or Not,"* pp. 100–101, 110–111, 212n. Forrest McDonald discusses demagoguery in the 1780s in *Novus Ordo Seclorum: The Intellectual Origins of the Constitution* (University Press of Kansas, 1985), pp. 164–165. He relates Hume's views on inertia on p. 161. Richard Hofstadter's analysis may be found in *Anti-Intellectualism in American Life* (Vintage Books, 1963), pp. 155–157. Al Gore defends reason in *The Assault on Reason* (Penguin Press, 2007). George Soros's beliefs are cited in Matt Bai, *The Argument: Billionaires, Bloggers, and the Battle to Remake Democratic Politics* (Penguin Press, 2007), p. 52. Frank Rich's comment is made in this *New York Times* column: "The 'Good Germans' Among Us," October 14, 2007 (www.nytimes.com/2007/10/14/opinion/14rich2.html?_r =2&oref=slogin&ref=opinion&pagewanted=print&oref=slogin). Eric Alterman's observation is made at the Huffington Post blog, November 9, 2006 (www.huffingtonpost.com/eric-alter man/31591495-strong_b_33770.html). Stanley Greenberg's analysis is in *The Two Americas* (Thomas Dunne Books, 2005), pp. 3–5, 20. The definition of conservatism in Clinton Rossiter's *Conservatism in America* (Knopf, 1962) is on p. 15. H. L. Mencken's quotation is cited by Bryan Caplan in *The Myth of the Rational Voter*, p. 18. William F. Buckley Jr.'s quotation is from *Up from Liberalism* (Banton, 1968), p. 104. He cites the comment by Albert Jay Nock on p. 101. Buckley's comment about the *National Review* is excerpted in *Conservatism in America Since 1930: A Reader*, ed. Gregory L. Schneider (New York University Press, 2003), p. 201. John Patrick Diggins's observation about Reagan is on p. 50 of his biography. Paul Weyrich's quotation is cited in Schneider's *Conservatism in America Since 1930*, p. 429.

CODA: HOPE

John Dewey predicts that consumers may make bad voters in *The Public and Its Problems* (1927; rpt. Swallow Press/Ohio University Press, 1954), p. 137.

Index

◆

reflecting public's denial of
problems, 124–127
shortcomings of televised
news, 110–113
televised political news
coverage, 112–114, 199
viewers' news habits, 17, 26
See also Advertising;
Television
Media Matters for America, 5
Meet the Press, 8, 103
Mencken, H. L., 162
Mendell, David, 194
Meyssan, Thierry, 130
Micklethwait, John, 159
Miers, Harriet, 49
Miller, Zell, 154
Mondale, Walter, 40, 51–52,
122–123
Moore, Michael, 144
Moral Majority, 167–168
Morris, Dick, 154
Morris, Edmund, 120
Mossadegh, Mohammad, 138
Moynihan, Daniel Patrick, 165
Mr. Smith Goes to Washington,
145
Murrow, Edward R., 103
Muslims, 130–131, 133, 134,
137
Myths, 53–66
about Lincoln, 58–59, 145

about Obama and McCain,
196–199
Bush's use of common man,
62–63
candidates of The People,
60–63
following 9/11, 133
log cabin, 57, 58
9/11, 137–138
power and uses of, 11–12
rags-to-riches theme of,
59–60
reluctance to confront, 142
role in U.S. politics, 53–54
The People, 2–3, 11, 63–66
voters' acceptance of, 2–3

Nader, Ralph, 153
Nasser, Gamal Abdel, 137
National Annenberg Election
Survey, 21, 108–109
National Election Studies
(NES), 18, 25–26
National Endowment for the
Arts, 29
National Public Radio, 7, 27
National Review, 164, 180
National security threats, 25
NBC, 96, 97
NBC Nightly News, 70
New York Post, 90